THE COTTAGE

BY SANDY RUSTIN

SIGNATURE ACTING EDITION

DPS | DRAMATISTS PLAY SERVICE, INC.

BROADWAY LICENSING GLOBAL

THE COTTAGE
Copyright © 2023, Sandy Rustin

All Rights Reserved

NOTE ON BILLING

Anyone receiving permission to produce THE COTTAGE is required to give credit to the Author as sole and exclusive Author of the Play on the title page of all programs distributed in connection with performances of the Play and in all instances in which the title of the Play appears, including printed or digital materials for advertising, publicizing or otherwise exploiting the Play and/or a production thereof. Please see your production license for font size and typeface requirements.

Be advised that there may be additional credits required in all programs and promotional material. Such language will be listed under the "Additional Billing" section of production licenses. It is the licensee's responsibility to ensure any and all required billing is included in the requisite places, per the terms of the license.

SPECIAL NOTE ON SONGS/RECORDINGS

Broadway Licensing neither holds the rights to nor grants permission to use any songs or recordings mentioned in the Play. Permission for performances of copyrighted songs, arrangements or recordings mentioned in this Play is not included in our license agreement. The permission of the copyright owner(s) must be obtained for any such use. For any songs and/or recordings mentioned in the Play, other songs, arrangements, or recordings may be substituted provided permission from the copyright owner(s) of such songs, arrangements or recordings is obtained; or songs, arrangements or recordings in the public domain may be substituted.

The original Broadway production of THE COTTAGE was produced by Broadway & Beyond Theatricals, Cornice Productions, Martian Entertainment, Paige Price, Scott Mauro, Malcolm Gosling/ Dan Gottfried, Gayle Seay/Tony Nation, Cornice Productions Fund 1, Michael Saperstein, Rick Costello, Jonathan Demar, Paul Jungquist, Tom & Judy Kleinman, Marjorie Morrissey, Mark Reardon, Shapiro Jensen Productions, Nina Tassler, Dale & James Young, and 7Sennotts LLC, opening in July 2023. It was directed by Jason Alexander, the scenic design was by Paul Tate dePoo III, the costume design was by Sydney Maresca, the lighting design was by Jiyoun Chang, the sound design was by Justin Ellington, the wig and hair design was by Tommy Kurzman, the dialect coach was Jerome Butler, and the production stage manager was lark hackshaw. The cast was as follows:

SYLVIA .... Laura Bell Bundy
BEAU .... Eric McCormack
MARJORIE .... Lilli Cooper
CLARKE .... Alex Moffat
DIERDRE .... Dana Steingold
RICHARD .... Nehal Joshi
UNDERSTUDIES .... Michelle Federer, Matthew Floyd Miller,
Tony Roach, Jamie Ann Romero

CHARACTERS

SYLVIA
A lovely and rash romantic.

BEAU
Perhaps the best-looking man in Britain.

MARJORIE
Eight months pregnant, pragmatic, and a tad spicy.

CLARKE
A distinguished gent with a lover's spirit.

DIERDRE
An awfully pretty, sometimes wise, nincompoop.

RICHARD
A murderous, yet gentle soul.

THE COTTAGE companies should strive to support a cast and crew of diverse theater workers. This diversity includes, but is not limited to, gender identities, ethnic and racial backgrounds, sexual orientations, body types, ages, and ability.

TIME

The play begins just before 9 A.M. Monday, June 4, 1923.

PLACE

A quaint family-owned cottage in the English countryside, about ninety minutes outside of London.

SET

The interior of the cottage.

NOTES

THE COTTAGE is a romantic and (not quite) murderous comedy of manners. The pacing is intended to be very swift. This script maps out suggested physicality in some cases, but casts are encouraged to embrace the style and find their own moments of doors swinging, cigarette lighting, and a general air of farce, while maintaining a truthful intention throughout.

Characters are often on separate wavelengths, experiencing the same moment in dramatically different ways. Discovering the abrupt beat changes is all part of the fun. Some are clearly marked, others are to be found as you go.

In this script, only the drawing room and staircase are visible. Designers should, however, feel free to imagine a visible foyer, bedroom, guest room, upstairs hall, kitchen and bathroom doors, etc. Space can be defined by budget and imagination.

Standard British dialect should be adhered to. Actresses playing Dierdre (Deer-drah) have the liberty of slowly descending into a lower-class dialect (Deer-dree). The words "Mama" and "Papa" should be pronounced per the French pronunciation, with accent over the final "a."

THE COTTAGE may be performed without an intermission, however no cuts may be made to the script.

"It is discouraging how many people are shocked by honesty and how few by deceit."

—Noël Coward

THE COTTAGE

ACT ONE

It's a glorious Monday morning in June 1923. Lights rise on a lovely cottage in the English countryside. Sunlight streams through the large bay windows. Remnants from an obviously passionate, desperately romantic evening (articles of clothing) are scattered across the set. Music plays on the Victrola.

Sylvia enters with a breakfast tray and sets it perfectly. Beneath her flowing, dramatic robe, she wears a glamorous negligee.

The sound of water running is heard from the bathroom offstage.

SYLVIA. *(Calling up hopefully.)* Beau, are you nearly through?

    No answer.

No matter.

    Sylvia continues to ready the breakfast and herself.

    She notices the window boxes and gets an idea. She quickly crosses and plucks a small yellow tulip. She fixes it behind her ear. Yes! Now she looks quite perfect!

    The water shuts off.

    Quickly, she finds a romantic posture and lies intentionally draped and gorgeous on the sofa. Perhaps she even dangles some grapes from the fruit basket above her mouth.

    Moments pass. It becomes difficult to hold her pose.

    The water turns back on.

    Frustrated, Sylvia breaks her pose…

(Calling up.) Beau are you nearly through?

BEAU. *(From the bathroom.)* What?

> *Buoyed, now that he's responded, she runs to the bottom of the stairs (or to the wing) and calls off to him more pointedly.*

SYLVIA. I say *(Water shuts off—less loudly.)* are you nearly through?

BEAU. *(From off.)* Quite.

SYLVIA. Good.

> *Hopeful that his entrance is imminent, she races back to her pose as she calls off romantically…*

(As the water turns back on.) I miss you!

> *Just as she gets back to her pose…*

BEAU. *(From off.)* What?

> *He can't hear her at all! She starts back to the bottom of the stairs…*

SYLVIA. *(Calling off, loudly.)* I say *(Water shuts off—less loudly.)* I miss you!

> *The sound of a door shutting is heard. He's on his way!*
>
> *In seemingly one leap, Sylvia lands miraculously back on the sofa in her original pose, grapes and all, albeit slightly less perfect than originally intended.*
>
> *Just missing Sylvia's perfect leap and return to casual elegance, Beau appears. He is tall, charming, and handsome. He wears a deep red silk robe and towels his hair.*

BEAU. Ah—just as I left you. Gorgeous. My gorgeous tulip.

SYLVIA. *(Regaining composure.)* Am I?

> *Beau enters fully now.*

BEAU. You know you are, darling. Why just now you've set yourself up perfectly to look coy and lovely, so that it would be exceedingly difficult for me to get properly dressed without distraction.

SYLVIA. Ah, darling. How well you know me.

BEAU. Do I?

SYLVIA. I love it when you call me Tulip.

BEAU. *(Oozing sex.)* Tulip.

SYLVIA. *(Euphorically.)* Ahhh.

10

He turns to go. Sylvia quickly shifts from orgasmic to desperate.
(Pleading.) Don't.

BEAU. Don't what?

SYLVIA. *(With renewed come-hitherness.)* Please don't get dressed. We've only just begun.

BEAU. Just begun? Good Lord, Sylvia, if that was just the beginning I'm afraid I'm not quite up to the task of making it to the end.

SYLVIA. Let's test you and find out.

> *They kiss passionately.*

I *wish* you were my husband.

BEAU. No you don't.

SYLVIA. Yes I do.

> *He kisses her (neck, ears, etc.), continuing foreplay through-*
> *out their dialogue.*

BEAU. If I were your husband you would despise me just as you despise Clarke and you would spend your evenings wishing to make love to him and not me.

SYLVIA. Do you really think so?

BEAU. I do.

SYLVIA. Well that's not very romantic, is it?

BEAU. Romance, my dear, is for fairy tales. This is not a romance. *(Getting sexier.)* This is sex.

SYLVIA. Passionate, wildly erotic sex.

BEAU. *(Sexier still.)* Un-wifely sex.

SYLVIA. Haven't you ever had wild sex with Marjorie?

> *The moment's now ruined. He breaks out of her embrace,*
> *releasing her haphazardly.*

BEAU. Marjorie's not in the mood for wild sex.

SYLVIA. Ever?

BEAU. Well, I suppose once when we were in the South of France, she let me…

SYLVIA. *(Interrupting.)* Never mind, darling, I don't want to know. *(Then.)* Do you feel guilty?

11

BEAU. For sleeping with you?

SYLVIA. Yes.

BEAU. No.

SYLVIA. *(Elated.)* Neither do I! I feel like I deserve to make love like I make love to you. And Clarke certainly doesn't do it, so I have no other choice but to turn to you.

BEAU. Is that a compliment?

SYLVIA. I'd say. If I really want to be made love to, Beau, I must come to you. And so I have—for one night, every summer, for seven summers.

BEAU. Has it been seven already? *(Distracted by the food.)* This looks lovely. Thank you Sylvie.

SYLVIA. Coffee?

BEAU. Please.

> *Sylvia pours and sugars the coffee demonstratively. Beau goes about his breakfast.*

SYLVIA. Somehow it lasts me, you know? This one night of spectacular *(Raises the spout spectacularly.)* lovemaking will see me through another year of rare and mediocre sex with Clarke.

> *She plops a sugar cube in the cup.*

BEAU. I don't take sugar.

SYLVIA. Don't you?

BEAU. 'Fraid not.

SYLVIA. *(As she quickly removes the sugar from his cup, putting it back—now wet—in the sugar bowl.)* Of course. Sorry. It's been so long.

> *She hands him the coffee, sans sugar.*

BEAU. You were saying?

SYLVIA. *(Back on track.)* Ah, yes. That our one night together will make up for all our nights apart.

BEAU. Will it?

SYLVIA. Of course. When I've no choice but to lie in bed with

Clarke, I simply close my eyes and imagine *us*—here, at this perfect cottage. My most favorite place in all the world.

BEAU. You sound like Mama.

SYLVIA. Do I? *(Then.)* Oh, I *love* it here. I always feel like I belong.

BEAU. As do I.

SYLVIA. I picture us in that bed of satin sheets, with window boxes of tulips; and that alone will bring me to climax.

BEAU. Will it?

SYLVIA. *(Dropping the sexy playfulness.)* Will you stop saying "will it" like that? You make me feel foolish.

BEAU. Not at all. You're not a bit foolish. You're wonderful and beautiful. When did you put that flower in your hair?

SYLVIA. *(Restoring the sexy playfulness.)* While you were washing up. I thought it would make me look fetching.

BEAU. It does. What else do you do while I'm washing up?

> *Spinning on a dime, brandishing a cigarette, Sylvia deflects the question without missing a beat.*

SYLVIA. Ciggy?

> *Note: Cigarettes, lighters, and ashtrays are always found throughout the cottage in the most unexpected places. (Think of a flower vase that's actually a cigarette holder, or a ceramic statue of David that's actually a cigarette holder—with a removable penis that's actually a lighter.) People are always taking one puff and then putting their cigarettes out to make a point.*
>
> *Note about the note: It isn't that cigarettes are hidden in unusual places, but rather, that typical objects have been unusually fashioned into cigarette holders.*

BEAU. No thank you, darling, I'm through with smoking.

SYLVIA. But you smoked last night.

BEAU. I know, but this morning I'm through with it. It's exhausting as a practice.

> *Beau lights Sylvia's cigarette.*

SYLVIA. Exhausting how?

BEAU. Just the planning of it all. Do I want one now or later—or now *and* later? Have I brought enough with me? Will they have them where I'm going? Do I have enough lighter fluid?

> *Sylvia laughs.*

God, I love it when you laugh.

> *Sylvia laughs more pointedly.*

No, my sweet, I love it when you really laugh. A sincere laugh. Without pretense.

SYLVIA. *(Defeated.)* Good Lord, Beau, you make me self-conscious.

BEAU. Sorry, sweetheart.

SYLVIA. *(Ever hopeful once more.)* Am I?

BEAU. What?

SYLVIA. Am I your sweetheart?

BEAU. Indeed.

> *They kiss. The music that has been quietly playing on the Victrola has petered out.*

SYLVIA. Do you ever wonder what would have happened had I met you first?

BEAU. I don't need to wonder. I know.

SYLVIA. Oh good! I'm so curious! Tell me.

BEAU. We would have married.

SYLVIA. I knew it! If we had married, we'd be the picture of happiness!

> *They are snuggled side by side and look the very picture.*

BEAU. *(After a thought.)* I don't know.

SYLVIA. *(Hurt, though hard-pressed to break the tableau.)* Don't you?

> *Church bells ring to claim the hour. Nine A.M. As the distant bells ring, dialogue continues.*

BEAU. Well, it could be that if we'd married, you'd be here now having this conversation with Clarke instead of me.

SYLVIA. You think I was destined to have a lover?

BEAU. Anything's possible I suppose, though I'm not one to speak of destiny; too magical a topic for the likes of me.

> *As they speak, Beau gathers up articles of clothing that are strewn about.*

SYLVIA. But isn't that what we're discussing now? Destiny? Fate?

BEAU. Ah, my lovely Tulip, I haven't a clue about fate, really. I do however, *(Referencing the last bell.)* know about late.

SYLVIA. Late?

> *Beau tosses Sylvia one of her unmentionables found draped across the set. (A brazier, a stocking, etc.)*

BEAU. Yes, darling, you're late.

SYLVIA. Oh!

BEAU. You were supposed to be aboard the train half an hour ago. Sooner or later, I've got to get to work.

SYLVIA. But I don't want our night to end!

BEAU. And yet it has, darling.

SYLVIA. I've been having such fun pretending to be your wife.

BEAU. Is that what you're doing?

> *As she speaks, she flips the record over and begins the quiet underscore of music again, with a romantic flourish.*

SYLVIA. I've been imagining us forever happy in this cottage, making love every night like husbands and wives.

BEAU. *(Genuine.)* Do you make love to Clarke every night?

SYLVIA. Heavens no! I mean happy husbands and wives.

BEAU. Ah. I see. You're sweet Sylvie. Come here.

> *He drops his pile of clothing deliberately. They embrace and kiss passionately.*

SYLVIA. Oh, what a perfect Monday!

> *Beau releases Sylvia haphazardly once more.*

BEAU. I really must get dressed.

SYLVIA. *(Recovering.)* Alas. So you must.

> *Beau collects his clothing, towel, etc., and exits to get dressed. Sylvia finds confidence.*

(Calling off with gusto.) Beau, I've made a decision, darling.

BEAU. *(From offstage.)* Mmmm?

SYLVIA. *(As she stops the music.)* A decision about us.

BEAU. *(Popping his head back in.)* Is it so serious we must have silence?

SYLVIA. *(A joyful declaration.)* I'm leaving Clarke!

> *Beau chuckles and moves to exit again.*

Don't laugh. I'm leaving him, Beau. I can't bear it another moment.

BEAU. Oh, Sylvie. You are adorable.

> *He exits.*

SYLVIA. *(Calling off passionately.)* I love you, Beau!

> *His door slams shut.*

> *Sylvia drops her robe and calls off with great expectation.*

I've sent him a telegram.

> *He's back.*

BEAU. *(With sudden real interest.)* Sorry?

SYLVIA. Last night, after supper, you went to take a bath.

BEAU. Yes.

SYLVIA. I sent a wire.

BEAU. You really are busy while I'm in the loo.

SYLVIA. Kiss me!

> *She runs to him! He pecks her cautiously.*

BEAU. Saying what, precisely?

SYLVIA. What?

BEAU. The telegram?

SYLVIA. Ah yes. I said, "Clarke. Stop. In love with Beau. Stop. I'm leaving. Stop. Sorry, darling. Stop."

BEAU. What?

SYLVIA. *(Repeating her action precisely.)* It said, "Clarke. Stop. In love with Beau…"

BEAU and SYLVIA. *(She's reciting, he is not.)* Stop.

BEAU. *(Continuing on—cutting her off from continued recitation.)* No, no, I heard you the first time I just…

SYLVIA. *(On her own track.)* I feel so free! Haven't you noticed how free I've been? Last night? *(Coquettishly.)* And this morning?

BEAU. Yes, but I attributed that to my new cologne.

SYLVIA. *(Inhaling him.)* It is rather divine.

BEAU. Thank you. A telegram?

SYLVIA. *(Still breathing him in.)* Mmm-hmm.

BEAU. Really?

SYLVIA. *(Unable to get enough of him.)* It's true.

BEAU. You know, I think I will take a cigarette.

> *He breaks away from her and lights himself a cigarette. They are on opposite ends of an emotional spectrum.*

SYLVIA. *(Adoringly.)* I love it when you smoke. You look the picture of health.

BEAU. What time was it when I took that bath?

SYLVIA. Nearly ten, I'd say.

BEAU. So you think Clarke's received the telegram by now?

SYLVIA. I'd say so.

BEAU. He'll see red, Sylvia.

SYLVIA. Will he?

BEAU. A Baldwin Conservative. A believer in convention, finance, and God…

SYLVIA. I'm not sure he'll really mind.

BEAU. You're rather apathetic.

SYLVIA. No. I don't feel apathetic. I feel alive!

BEAU. You don't think your husband will mind that you've declared your love for another man—his *brother*?

> *A slight beat.*

SYLVIA. Well, when you put it like that.

BEAU. Is there another way to put it?

SYLVIA. Look, he might be a bit miffed, I'll give you that. But I doubt he'll truly mind.

BEAU. Doesn't he love you at all?

SYLVIA. Isn't it all or nothing?

BEAU. *(Turning away.)* I'm not sure.

SYLVIA. *(Turning away.)* Well then neither am I.

BEAU. *(Back into her.)* Still, darling…a telegram?

> *She goes to him. They're on different emotional tracks.*

SYLVIA. I can't live without you, Beau. I don't want to go another three hundred and sixty-four days dreaming of you, only to have one short-lived night over all too soon.

BEAU. How poetic.

SYLVIA. I know you want more than just one day with me per year.

BEAU. How well you know me.

SYLVIA. Beau, darling, you and I have been stuck in the wrong marriages.

BEAU. That may be so, Sylvie, but they are marriages nonetheless.

SYLVIA. True, but they needn't be an obstacle.

BEAU. You seem so sure.

SYLVIA. We're in love! What could be surer than that?

BEAU. Even still, a telegram's a rather cold way to make such an announcement, Sylvie.

SYLVIA. Oh I could never *face* Clarke. He gets all sweaty and pathetic-looking when he's upset.

BEAU. Ah! So you admit, he'll be upset.

SYLVIA. Perhaps a trifle. But darling, really it's you I can't bear to see upset.

> *Beau begins to clear the table, Sylvia at his heels. (If there's a swinging kitchen door, they are back and forth through the door. If no door, then they are back and forth through the exit as dialogue swiftly continues.)*

BEAU. Well, darling, then perhaps you could have mentioned this telegram to me before you'd sent it.

SYLVIA. You told me last night you like it when I "take charge."

BEAU. Context darling.

SYLVIA. This is perfect context! I'm taking charge of my life! I'm starting our lives anew!

BEAU. I'd argue that when Clarke arrives, our lives will be quite ended.

SYLVIA. But Clarke won't come here.

BEAU. Won't he?

SYLVIA. How could he? He's no idea where we are.

BEAU. Hasn't he?

SYLVIA. *(Smartly.)* I told him I was going to my aunt's in London.

BEAU. Ah. Did it occur to you that perhaps I speak to Clarke occasionally.

SYLVIA. *(This has not occurred to her.)* Sorry?

BEAU. I speak to my brother, occasionally. For example, Friday. He phoned to tell me about Mama's condition…

SYLVIA. Poor dear…

BEAU. *(Nearly an aside.)* Awful. *(Immediately moving on.)* And as we were hanging up he inquired about my weekend plans.

SYLVIA. Well surely, you didn't…

BEAU. "I'll be at the cottage," I told him. I assume he assumed I meant with Marjorie.

SYLVIA. I see. So you think that means he'll…

> *A knock at the door. Sylvia and Beau look out.*

BEAU. I do.

SYLVIA. Oh dear.

BEAU. And the pair of us still in our skivvies.

> *Sylvia desperately looks for a nook. Beau, tense, lights another cigarette.*

SYLVIA. *(And now a panic.)* Hide me! Where shall I hide?

BEAU. But why should he be upset if he doesn't love you?

SYLVIA. Because he's a man!

BEAU. I thought you said he won't mind.

SYLVIA. I thought *you* stopped smoking!

Beau extinguishes his cigarette. More knocking.

MARJORIE. *(From off.)* Beau?

Beau and Sylvia both look to the door.

(From off.) Beau, I know you're in there. Let me in.

BEAU. *(Whispered and unhinged.)* Marjorie? But how is she here?!

SYLVIA. *(Sheepishly.)* I may have sent a telegram to her as well.

BEAU. Oh, Sylvia.

SYLVIA. As your mother always says: "Best to kill two birds with one stone."

BEAU. My mother says a lot of things, Sylvia!

SYLVIA. Yes, but I'm the only one who listens.

BEAU. You've really upset the apple cart, haven't you?

SYLVIA. *(Dramatically.)* It needed upsetting, Beau.

MARJORIE. *(Cross knocking.)* Beau?! Open this door!

SYLVIA. *(Gently.)* Do you think she's cross?

BEAU. It's quite possible.

SYLVIA. I do hate confrontation.

BEAU. Love sending telegrams though, is that it?

More violent knocking interrupts.

MARJORIE. *(Over her knocking.)* I say, open this door!!!

SYLVIA. *(Desperate.)* Where shall I go?!

BEAU. Upstairs.

SYLVIA. So far away?

BEAU. The kitchen then.

SYLVIA. I won't be able to hear!

BEAU. Fine!

Beau opens the window seat to reveal a perfect hiding spot.

SYLVIA. Oh! How convenient!

BEAU. In you go.

Beau shoves her in gracelessly.

SYLVIA. Thank you, darling. *(Just before being closed in.)* Be brave!

The window seat cover slams shut. More knocking.

MARJORIE. *(From off.)* Beau!

More knocking.

Open this door. The charade is over.

BEAU. *(Calling off—perhaps pretending to be farther away than he is.)* Coming dear.

SYLVIA. *(Muffled, but clear, from within the window seat.)* I love you, Beau!

Beau deliberately places his wedding band (from his robe pocket) back on his finger, then opens the door. Wind blows, birds chirp. Marjorie enters. She is hugely pregnant.

MARJORIE. Thank you.

BEAU. Pleasure.

MARJORIE. Good morning.

BEAU. You're looking well.

MARJORIE. I feel well. What a smart robe.

BEAU. Thank you.

MARJORIE. *(Taking off her hat and gloves.)* I thought I'd find you here. This place always looks cheerful in the summer.

BEAU. Indeed it does. Did you walk here from the train?

MARJORIE. I hired a cab.

BEAU. Ah.

MARJORIE. *(Handing Beau her things.)* I always love it here.

BEAU. As do I.

MARJORIE. *(Touching her belly.)* It's a perfect family home.

BEAU. It is.

MARJORIE. Reminds me of our wedding day.

BEAU. Mmm.

MARJORIE. Now that was a beautiful day at the cottage, wasn't it?

BEAU. Indeed.

MARJORIE. S'pose that's all water under the bridge now.

BEAU. Is it?

MARJORIE. *(Finding Sylvia's undergarment.)* I'd say.

BEAU. *(Grabbing it from Marjorie—perhaps dusting off the seat with it.)* Have a seat.

MARJORIE. *(Pointed.)* I think I'll stand.

BEAU. Right. *(Tosses it—perhaps even into the crowd. Then.)* So, I understand you've received a telegram.

MARJORIE. Indeed.

> *A British moment.*

BEAU. Would you care for a cup of tea?

MARJORIE. Lovely.

> *Beau starts to go.*

Where is Mrs. Lorrey?

BEAU. Considering *my guest*, I couldn't very well have the servants here, now could I darling?

MARJORIE. Of course. *(Noticing Sylvia's robe.)* And where is… *your guest*?

BEAU. *(A moment and then a choice.)* Hiding in the window nook.

SYLVIA. *(Strained from within the nook.)* Beau?!!

BEAU. *(Loudly.)* Might as well come out and kill the first bird, Sylvie.

> *Marjorie opens the window seat and peers down.*

MARJORIE. Yes, Sylvie, please do come out.

> *Marjorie allows the seat cover to slam. Sylvia harrumphs from within. ("Ouch!") Beau helps Sylvia out.*

BEAU. Careful, darling.

MARJORIE. Good morning, Sylvie.

SYLVIA. *(Sheepishly as she climbs out.)* Good morning.

> *Sylvia, once out, notices and AUDIBLY GASPS at Marjorie's belly!*

MARJORIE. Quite.

SYLVIA. You're expecting?!

MARJORIE. July.

SYLVIA. Next month?!

MARJORIE. July is the very next month, yes.

SYLVIA. Beau! Did you know about this?!

BEAU. I should say so!

SYLVIA. But *I* never knew!

BEAU. You never asked.

SYLVIA. I…

MARJORIE. You should come for tea when I invite you.

SYLVIA. I suppose I should, but I worried it might be awkward.

MARJORIE. How sensitive of you.

SYLVIA. Does your mother know?!

BEAU. Hard to know what she knows these days.

MARJORIE. *(Handing her the robe.)* Lovely negligee darling.

SYLVIA. *(Putting her robe back on.)* It is, isn't it?

BEAU. Will you take tea, Sylvie?

SYLVIA. *(Still shocked.)* Yes, please.

    As Beau exits to get tea…

MARJORIE. Your telegram was rather startling, Sylvia.

SYLVIA. I'd say we're both a bit startled this morning.

MARJORIE. "I love Beau. Stop. Beau loves me. Stop. Sorry Marji."

MARJORIE and SYLVIA. *(With opposing intentions.)* "Stop."

    Beau pops his head back in.

BEAU. Milk? Sugar?

    The ladies respond intensely and then resume conversation.

MARJORIE and SYLVIA. Black.

BEAU. Of course.

    Beau retreats to the kitchen.

SYLVIA. Well, I wanted to get to the point.

MARJORIE. *(Pointedly.)* So you did.

SYLVIA. I didn't know you were pregnant!

MARJORIE. *(A bit of a confession.)* Not to worry, dear, this is actually quite convenient.

> *On the heels of the word "convenient," Beau enters with a tea tray from the kitchen AND there's a knock at the door. They all look out.*

Who's that?

> *Beau sets the tray down. More knocking.*

CLARKE. *(From off.)* Sylvie?

> *They all look at the door.*

MARJORIE. *(Gobsmacked.)* Clarke?

CLARKE. *(From off.)* Beau, I know you're in there. Open the door.

SYLVIA. Perhaps telegrams weren't such a grand idea after all.

BEAU. Delayed logic is consistently disappointing.

> *Beau wipes his brow with his hanky, then opens the door. Wind blows, birds chirp. Clarke enters.*

Good morning, Clarke.

CLARKE. Morning.

BEAU. How was your walk?

CLARKE. Lovely. *(Genuine.)* What a smart robe.

BEAU. It's from China.

CLARKE. *(Handing Beau his hat/umbrella.)* I didn't see any robes like that when I was in China.

BEAU. Well, next time you go I'll give you the name of the tailor.

CLARKE. Yes, please, I'd like that *(Feeling it.)* —silky, smooth… *(Noticing Marjorie and Sylvia.)* Darling?!

MARJORIE. Clarke!   **SYLVIA.** Clarke.

CLARKE. Darling, what are you doing here?

SYLVIA. Darling, you knew I was here. You came looking for me.

CLARKE. No, not you, darling. *(To Marjorie.)* You, darling.

MARJORIE. Did you get a telegram from Sylvie too then, darling? We must have been on the same train. What a relief, isn't it, dear?

CLARKE. Quite!

> *Sylvia and Beau look at each other, then back to Clarke and Marjorie.*

SYLVIA and BEAU. Sorry?

CLARKE. We haven't known how to tell you.

SYLVIA. Tell us what?

CLARKE. *(Genuine.)* That's a lovely negligee, Sylvie.

SYLVIA. Thank you, Clarke.

BEAU. Tell us what, Clarke?

CLARKE. *(Soaking in the place.)* I always love it here.

BEAU. As do I.

CLARKE. It's so tidy and well kept.

BEAU. Mother wouldn't have it any other way.

CLARKE. That's what *I'm* saying.

SYLVIA. Tell us what, Clarke?

CLARKE. Ah, yes. Simply put… *(Not at all simply.)* Marjorie and I are in love!

> *Clarke and Marjorie revel in their love.*
>
> *Note: Wherever Marjorie and Clarke can steal a kiss, a look, a grab, they ought to. There's nothing "mediocre" about what they have together.*

BEAU. With each other?

MARJORIE. Quite. In fact, Beau, darling, well, I suppose considering *your* news it will come as a comfort to you now. This child is not yours!

CLARKE. *(With enormous pride.)* I'm the father, Beau! *(Breathes deeply, now joyous.)* God, it feels good to get that off my chest! I was dreading having to act the uncle to my son.

MARJORIE. Or daughter.

CLARKE. *(A throwaway.)* Right. *(Now a proclamation.)* I want the child to call me Papa!

MARJORIE. What a favor you've done us, Sylvie! I know tonight,

I shall sleep well for once. It's been awful. Sneaking away at every chance we could. Loving in secret these long seven years.

SYLVIA and BEAU. Seven years?!

BEAU. *(Keeping a lid on it.)* I'm getting some ice.

    Beau moves toward the kitchen.

MARJORIE. Why?

BEAU. I think I'll have a scotch. Sylvie?

SYLVIA. *(Truly in need of one.)* Yes, please.

    Beau exits.

MARJORIE. At nine in the morning? How daring! *(Calling off.)* You know, I think I'll have one too!

CLARKE. *(Calling off.)* Make that four. *(Nuzzling Marjorie.)* It's a bit of a celebration isn't it?

SYLVIA. Seems debatable. *(To Marjorie.)* Sneaking away at *every* chance you could? As in—often?!

MARJORIE. No more often than you and Beau, I'm sure.

SYLVIA. We limit ourselves to one night per year.

    A beat and then Clarke and Marjorie burst out laughing.

MARJORIE. One night?!

CLARKE. That's quite disciplined!

SYLVIA. *(With seething incredulousness.)* Yes, well, we're married, you see, so we felt the impropriety was best handled in a moderated capacity!

    Beau enters with ice.

BEAU. *(Still heated.)* Ice!

    Beau fixes drinks at the bar.

MARJORIE. *(With a twinkle in her eye.)* We weren't able to have that kind of self-control.

SYLVIA. Weren't you?

MARJORIE. I've never felt so alive as I do when I'm with Clarke.

BEAU. Lovely.

CLARKE. It has been rather exciting.

Clarke and Marjorie canoodle.

SYLVIA. *(To Clarke.)* And here, I thought you spent your spare time at the library.

MARJORIE. Mm, yes. The library, the study… *(With an extra twinkle.)* …the stables.

SYLVIA and BEAU. The stables?!

Marjorie and Clarke revel in the memory.

SYLVIA. *(Disgustedly.)* Where did you do it? Were the horses watching?

MARJORIE. Oh, what difference does it make where? Whether one night or every night, an affair's an affair, isn't it?

SYLVIA and BEAU. Every night?!

CLARKE. *(Utterly casual, to Sylvia.)* Well, not every night, darling. Some nights I really *did* have to work.

MARJORIE. Perhaps God simply got mixed up and put the wrong brother with the wrong wife.

BEAU. *(Handing out drinks.)* Let's not bring God into this, shall we?

CLARKE. And why not? With the way I feel about Marjorie, I see no other explanation!

MARJORIE. Oh Clarke.

CLARKE. *(Another proclamation.)* A higher power has brought us together!

MARJORIE. How glorious!

Clarke and Marjorie kiss.

CLARKE. Cheers!

They clink glasses.

ALL. *(Emotionally diverse.)* Cheers!

They sip. Then…

SYLVIA. *(To Beau.)* Beau, if my husband and your wife have been together every evening, where have you been? You told me we couldn't see each other but once a year or Marjorie would suspect you.

Beau pours himself another.

But if Marjorie's…in the stables…then it seems to me you should be the one suspicious of her. When Clarke's not home, he tells me he's at work. What excuse does Marjorie give you?

MARJORIE. I don't.

SYLVIA. What?

MARJORIE. I don't need to give an excuse, Sylvie. He's never home either.

SYLVIA. He's never…

> *A knock at the door. All look out.*

DIERDRE. *(From off, with doubtless hope and unrelenting romanticism.)* Beau?!

> *They all look at the door.*

Beau! It's me, darling! Please open the door!

> *A small beat.*

BEAU. Damn.

> *Beau drinks. Dierdre knocks more.*

DIERDRE. *(From off.)* Beau, I have the most wonderful news! Are you there?

SYLVIA. Who's that?!

BEAU. That will be Dierdre.

MARJORIE. Who?

BEAU. Dierdre. My lover.

SYLVIA. *(Floored.)* Your lover?! Then who am I?

MARJORIE. *(Nearly giddy from the scandal.)* Who indeed?

BEAU. You are my sister-in-law and we share one night a year together.

SYLVIA. What?!

MARJORIE. *(Ever the detective.)* I knew you had a lover! I knew it.

BEAU. I'm so glad you're pleased, dear.

CLARKE. My my, Beau, this does come as a bit of a shock. I didn't know you had it in you.

MARJORIE. You speak of it as though it's something to be proud of Clarke!

28

CLARKE. No, no. I'm just surprised, that's all.

SYLVIA. Well that makes two of us!

MARJORIE. I'm surprised too. So really, it's three.

DIERDRE. *(Still at the door.)* I have a *surprise* for you!

MARJORIE. Oh goody. A theme!

DIERDRE. *(Still at the door.)* I can hardly wait another moment! Please open the door!

SYLVIA. *(Imitating.)* Yes, "*please.*"

> *Beau deliberately takes his wedding ring back off, then opens the door. Wind blows, birds chirp. Dierdre, a sweet young optimist, enters with more bags than she can comfortably carry. As they talk, Beau helps her with her bags, hat, etc.*

DIERDRE. Beau, I had to see you! Oooh, what a lovely robe!

BEAU. Thank you, darling.

DIERDRE. *(Delighted.)* I didn't expect a costume! I've got my kimono in one of these bags. We can play "all aboard the Orient Express" later.

BEAU. Brilliant.

DIERDRE. *(Breathing in the day.)* I'm so glad to be here! Without you leading the way, I got a bit lost on the walk from the train! Oh! I love this cottage!

BEAU. As do I.

DIERDRE. It always feels a bit naughty.

> *She kisses him naughtily.*

Your secretary told me you'd be here.

SYLVIA. You told your secretary?!

DIERDRE. *(Suddenly noticing everyone.)* Oh! Hello, everyone. I didn't expect a party. Will there be games?

MARJORIE. Seems we're in the middle of one.

DIERDRE. *(Genuine.)* What a lovely negligee.

SYLVIA. Thank you.

> *Sylvia pointedly gets a cigarette from another unlikely spot.*

BEAU. Dierdre, allow me to introduce you. This is my brother, Clarke.

DIERDRE. *(Honored.)* Pleased to meet you.

BEAU. My wife, Marjorie.

DIERDRE. *(Shocked.)* Your wife?! But…

> *Marjorie reveals her belly to Dierdre.*

MARJORIE. How do you do?

DIERDRE. *(Audibly gasping at the belly.)* Beau!

BEAU. And my sister-in-law, Sylvia.

SYLVIA. Your sister-in-law? That's how you introduce me? *(To Dierdre—dramatically blowing smoke.)* Hello, dear. *I* am Beau's lover!

CLARKE and MARJORIE. *(Applauding Sylvia's presentation.)* Brava!

DIERDRE. *(Thoroughly confused and a bit blinded by the smoke.)* Sorry?

BEAU. *(To Dierdre.)* Don't worry, darling, it's just one night per year.

DIERDRE. What?

SYLVIA. Just? Just! I'll tell you, in that one night, we make love more fervently than all the lovers in the world put together.

CLARKE. *(Sharing a moment with Marjorie.)* That's a bit difficult to prove, Sylvie, don't you think?

DIERDRE. It is.

SYLVIA. Beau, what is the meaning of this…this…girl?

DIERDRE. *(Figuring it all out.)* Oh! Is *this* the game?

BEAU. Afraid so.

DIERDRE. Oh! How do I play?

BEAU. Darling, you came to tell me something urgent, did you not?

DIERDRE. Oh! I did, yes. But, now, in light of present company, perhaps…

MARJORIE. Oh please, Dierdre, we're family. Don't let us spoil your plans.

DIERDRE. Right. Well—I…

She absolutely would continue, if it weren't for Clarke's enthusiasm.

CLARKE. Out with it, dear.

DIERDRE. Well—I…

CLARKE. You'll feel so much better once it's out.

DIERDRE. Well—I…

CLARKE. I know I do!

SYLVIA. Will you let the girl speak?

MARJORIE. Touchy, Sylvie.

SYLVIA. Go on, Dierdre, what have you come to tell us?

DIERDRE. Oh! Yes, well, I wanted to say, I've got my divorce finalized. The papers came this morning. So—Beau, we're free to marry!

MARJORIE and CLARKE. Divorce?!   **SYLVIA.** Marry?!

CLARKE. *(On the heels of the above.)* Oh really, Beau. What a scandal!

MARJORIE. *(On the word "scandal.")* You've attached yourself to a divorcée? Beau, I'm shocked.

SYLVIA. *(On the word "divorcée.")* Are you marrying this girl?

BEAU. *(Silencing them.)* Just a moment all of you.

　　　　A British moment.

Dierdre darling, would you like a cup of tea?

DIERDRE. Am I staying?

MARJORIE. Yes, please do, stay. We were raised Anglican.

CLARKE. We've never chatted with a divorcée.

DIERDRE. It's only been two hours.

CLARKE and MARJORIE. Good enough.

DIERDRE. *(Happily settled.)* Right!

BEAU. Tea then?

DIERDRE. *(Ever cheerful.)* Mmm-hmm.

BEAU. Lovely.

　　　　Beau exits to get more tea. Marjorie, Clarke, and Dierdre make themselves comfortable.

MARJORIE. Now tell us, is it difficult to get a divorce?

DIERDRE. Well…

CLARKE. *(Interrupting.)* Did Beau arrange it for you?

DIERDRE. Well…

MARJORIE. *(Interrupting.)* Because now, with a baby and all—

CLARKE. *(A quick canoodle.) Our* baby…finally an heir to the Van Kipness…

SYLVIA. *(Cutting Clarke off, urgently.)* Pardon me, everybody…

> *They all look at Sylvia.*

…but if I've done my calculations correctly, it appears that quite suddenly I am the odd man out.

CLARKE. *(Dismissively.)* Quite right, darling. It does seem that way, doesn't it?

MARJORIE. Well, perhaps that's fair considering you were the one who sent the telegrams.

DIERDRE. What telegrams?

SYLVIA. Fair? Fair! All this time, I thought I was the one being risqué and dangerous. Turns out, I'm the conservative of this bunch, aren't I? *(To Marjorie.)* Pregnant by your husband's brother? *(To Clarke.)* And you—impregnating your brother's wife! *(To Dierdre.)* You—you're barely grown and already flaunting divorce papers in front of your lover's lover and his pregnant wife.

> *Beau enters with tea.*

BEAU. Tea?

SYLVIA. *(Spinning to face Beau furiously.)* And you! Unfaithful to the one you're being unfaithful with! How dare you? It's despicable! All of you!

> *Sylvia moves to exit to the bedroom.*

BEAU. You seem awfully comfortable doling out blame, Sylvie.

SYLVIA. *(Stopping herself.)* Haven't I earned the right?

BEAU. I don't know. We may be in a bit of a jam here, but I'd say you're the one smack dab in the middle of it, and therefore haven't quite the right to judge it.

Sylvia crosses back in, fuming.

SYLVIA. Oh! Oh?! I can't judge the jam?!

MARJORIE. *(Casually.)* I'd love some jam, thank you, I'm starving.

SYLVIA. There's crumpets in the kitchen. Help yourself.

Marjorie audibly and physically struggles to get up from the sofa.

Oh, never mind, don't strain yourself, Marji. Perhaps I'll find some clarity in the kitchen!!

Sylvia exits disgustedly to the kitchen.

MARJORIE. *(Calling off.)* Thank you, Sylvie. Even in times of stress, you really are such a dear.

The sound of Sylvia (intentionally?) dropping a tray in the kitchen is heard.

CLARKE. *(Calling off.)* Sylvie?

SYLVIA. *(Angrily from the kitchen.)* I'm fine!

CLARKE. *(Calling off.)* Just checking.

Note: Each time one of these onstage/offstage exchanges between Clarke and Sylvia appear, Clarke's lines are to sound authoritative, yet rather inconclusive. Musically speaking, the intonation on these shouted lines goes up at the end.

Marjorie pats the seat next to her.

MARJORIE. Dierdre, do sit down! *(From yet another uncommon source.)* Cigarette?

DIERDRE. Oh, no thank you. I don't smoke.

CLARKE. No?

DIERDRE. My husband doesn't approve.

MARJORIE. Well, really, that's no matter now, eh? *(Offering a cigarette.)* Go on.

DIERDRE. I suppose you're right! Thank you.

Clarke lights their cigarettes as...

MARJORIE. So, tell us, what's it like to be a divorcée?

DIERDRE. Dunno yet. I've only just got the papers.

MARJORIE. But what did your husband do when you told him?

33

DIERDRE. *(An enormous realization.)* Oh.

MARJORIE. What?

> *Dierdre suddenly puts out her cigarette and nervously begins to pace.*

BEAU. My dear, are you quite alright?

DIERDRE. No, no I'm afraid I'm not at all alright.

> *Dierdre begins to cry.*

MARJORIE. Oh dear!

CLARKE. Are you unwell?

BEAU. Dierdre, darling, what's the matter?

DIERDRE. Well, that's just it. I haven't got round to telling you about Richard!

BEAU. What about him?

DIERDRE. I was so excited about the papers, and being free to marry you—the man I know in my heart of hearts I was truly meant to marry—that I forgot to mention Richard.

BEAU. Heart of hearts, yes, yes, what do you want to say?

DIERDRE. It's too awful.

> *Sylvia enters with a plate of crumpets and jam.*

CLARKE. It's the anticipation that makes it awful. Reality is never quite as glum.

SYLVIA. Here you are, Marjorie, wouldn't want you to starve…

MARJORIE. Oooo! Yummy! Thank you Sylvie!

> *Marjorie begins to eat ravenously. Dierdre lets out a sob.*

SYLVIA. What's this? My lover's lover is crying? What's the matter, darling? Did you find another woman in the broom closet?

> *Dierdre lets out another slightly bigger sob.*

Or is your sister-in-law carrying your husband's baby?

> *Dierdre lets out the biggest sob of all.*

BEAU. This may come as a shock to you, Sylvia, but this particular moment is not about you. *(Tenderly to Dierdre.)* There, there, dear.

SYLVIA. *(To herself.)* It's amazing how twenty minutes can completely change how one feels about a person.

CLARKE. *(To Dierdre.)* Go on, dear, you can tell us.

BEAU. Please, Petunia—whatever it is, we'll deal with it.

SYLVIA. Petunia? Petunia?! Is that what you call her?!

MARJORIE. That is rather gauche Beau, darling, seeing as you've always called me Daisy.

SYLVIA. What, do you just go round naming ladies after flowers?

> *She throws the tulip on the ground in protest.*

Here I was thinking Tulip was so romantic.

BEAU. I told you—what we had was not a romance.

MARJORIE. *(Referring to the crumpets.)* These are delicious, Sylvie. Did you make them?

SYLVIA. *(Irate.)* I did. And I am never giving you the recipe!

> *Sylvia takes a drink.*
>
> *Dierdre blows her nose loudly in a hanky Clarke has provided.*

DIERDRE. *(Handing the hanky back to Clarke.)* Thanks.

CLARKE. Keep it.

> *Dierdre wails with renewed spirit.*

MARJORIE. Alright then, darling Petunia, what is so upsetting?

BEAU. Yes, darling, please tell us.

MARJORIE. Be honest.

DIERDRE. It's Richard.

SYLVIA. Who's Richard?

CLARKE, BEAU, and MARJORIE. Her husband.

DIERDRE. *(Through tears.)* Ex-husband.

> *Note: Throughout, whenever Dierdre (or later Richard) inserts an "ex-husband" as a correction, it is to be treated quite slightly. Almost as if it hasn't been inserted at all.*

BEAU. Darling, what about Richard?

DIERDRE. He…he…he's going to kill you.

> *It has built to this moment and now…silence. Then, suddenly, Beau leading the way, they all begin to laugh. The tension of the morning has finally found its release.*

Their laughter grows until they're nearly crying. A true moment of familial connection.

While they're laughing, Dierdre tries several tactics to interrupt them, it is not until her last line that she is finally heard and their laughter is cut off.

(Over their growing laughter.) Stop it! Stop it, the lot of you! Why are you laughing? It's not funny! This is serious. He's quite large, you know. He has guns! Richard is a dangerous man. There's nothing funny about this! *He's killed all my other lovers!*

The laughter stops dead.

BEAU. What's that, darling?

DIERDRE. Richard. *(Rather sheepishly.)* He's killed all my other lovers.

SYLVIA. How many damn lovers do you people keep? Is nothing sacred?

DIERDRE. *(A quote she's heard.)* "One's love is only sacred, if one has had the good fortune of actually discovering one's truest and intended love."

All look at Dierdre.

SYLVIA. You're full of surprises, aren't you?

DIERDRE. Oh dear! Please don't tell.

MARJORIE. Tell whom?

DIERDRE. The police or something. I wouldn't want him to get into trouble.

CLARKE. For killing people?!?

DIERDRE. Mmm. It's my fault really. I'm the one having the affairs.

SYLVIA. You're taking the blame for your husband's…

DIERDRE. Ex-husband's…

SYLVIA. …Ex-husband's murders?

BEAU. Dierdre, darling. Are you saying your husband, Richard, is a murderer?

DIERDRE. Ex-husband, truly, and well, I don't like to put it that way. "Murderer" has such *negative connotations*, doesn't it? But— um—yes, well—yes—he's—he's got a *nasty temper.*

36

CLARKE. Our mother has a nasty temper, she's a bitch; not a murderer.

BEAU. Leave Mother out of this.

SYLVIA. You want to leave everyone out of this don't you?! *(A list.)* Your mother…me…God…

> *Characteristic sibling rivalry builds.*

CLARKE. I was simply using Mother for example.

BEAU. Well, don't. We are, after all, in her home.

CLARKE. *(Sarcastic.)* Sor-ry, Beau.

BEAU. In consideration of Mama's current condition, I imagine she should be quite far from the butt of jokes, don't you agree?

CLARKE. Now you sound like Father.

BEAU. May he rest in peace.

CLARKE. Of course.

BEAU. Well someone needs to be the man of this family!

CLARKE. What's that supposed to mean?!

MARJORIE. *(Interrupting their spat.)* Boys! Help me up!

> *Beau and Clarke struggle to do so, ad-libbing. ("Sorry, dear," "Oh! Of course," etc.)*

Dierdre, does Richard know where you've gone?

DIERDRE. *(Considering herself wise.)* I left him a note.

BEAU. A farewell note?

DIERDRE. I had to leave a forwarding address, didn't I? What about my mail?

SYLVIA. *(Nearly to herself.)* And do you get a lot of mail?

BEAU. *(On the heels of the above.)* So you gave him *this* address?

DIERDRE. Oh, no, don't be daft, darling. I gave him your office address.

BEAU. My office?

DIERDRE. I figure, he can't hurt you there, because you're here!

BEAU. So I am.

As Beau goes to the telephone and dials, Sylvia turns to a taxidermized animal...

SYLVIA. Is this a real moment or am I hallucinating?

CLARKE. Who are you calling?

BEAU. Yes, Operator. Get me Picadilly-342 please.

DIERDRE. But that's your office number.

BEAU. It is.

CLARKE. But you're not there.

BEAU. It's Monday morning, Clarke. Lawyers have secretaries. It's the wave of the future.

CLARKE. *(Defensive.)* Accountants have secretaries too!

MARJORIE. *(Comforting.)* Of course they do, dear.

DIERDRE. Your secretary! Oh my! I didn't think of that. You don't think she'd tell him, do you?

BEAU. How *big* is he?

DIERDRE. Oh dear. Oh dear!

> *Clarke goes to the bar to fix drinks. Dierdre goes to the window to look for Richard.*

MARJORIE. Now, calm down, Dierdre. Beau is very pragmatic. He'll handle it.

> *The pace and focus now shift to Beau.*

BEAU. *(Into the phone, ever the professional.)* Yes, hello, Mrs. Worthington. Calling for my messages. *(Then.)* I see.

> *They all lean in, curious.*

Well, please tell Mr. Jasper I'll do my best to file the appeal by Wednesday morning.

> *They relax.*

Was he?

> *They lean in, curious again—then he shares with them...*

Mr. Jasper's second son was accepted to Eton as a late transfer.

> *They all motion to hurry it up—he's back to the phone.*

Bravo, bravo—uh—anything else, dear? Did anybody...pop by?

They lean in slightly.

A man?

They lean in slightly more.

A large man?

DIERDRE. Oh dear, oh dear!

Dierdre moves to a better vantage point.

BEAU. He wanted to know where he could find me. Did you tell him? Of course, you did. No, no, it wasn't a secret.

SYLVIA. It wasn't?!

BEAU. It's perfectly fine that you told him.

DIERDRE. Perfectly fine?!

BEAU. What time would you say the fellow dropped by? First thing this morning.

DIERDRE. He must have been right behind me.

Dierdre begins to gather her things with great difficulty.

BEAU. Right then. Well, it's been nice knowing you, Mrs. Worthington.

Hmm?

Oh nothing, dear. Good day to you.

Beau hangs up the phone.

A beat. Then with desperation, he's off to ready himself for immediate departure.

During the following dialogue, Beau manages to get dressed.

He moves on and off stage as he gathers his clothes from last night's tryst—a shirt in the kitchen, a sock in the guest room, etc., appearing at just the right moment for his dialogue, each time having found another article of clothing and/or in varying stages of undress.

DIERDRE. Beau, this is terrible news. Richard must be on his way here. He has guns, Beau. Many different kinds of guns. Small ones. Big ones…

Clarke hands Dierdre a drink.

CLARKE. Drink?

DIERDRE. *(Very much wanting the drink.)* Oh, no thank you.

> *She hands it back—Clarke downs it.*

Richard doesn't like me to drink.

SYLVIA. Does he prefer you to kill people?

CLARKE. *(With morbid curiosity.)* Dierdre, what has he done with the... *(Disgusted.)* ...you know...in the past?

DIERDRE. What do you mean?

CLARKE. With the... *(Nearly vomiting.)* ...bodies? After?

DIERDRE. *(With pride and fear.)* Oh. Different things. He's very creative.

MARJORIE. For example?

DIERDRE. *(Continuing her ghost story.)* Well, he buried one once.

MARJORIE. That's not creative.

DIERDRE. *(And still.)* No, he buried him in the cement of the back porch stairs.

SYLVIA. Better.	**MARJORIE.** There we are.	**CLARKE.** Well, that's ghastly, isn't it?

DIERDRE. *(And even still.)* And once he drowned a chap while pretending to be a lifeguard.

CLARKE. Brutal!

DIERDRE. Haven't even told you about bloody Harold!

> *She indicates a slice of the throat—they audibly react.*

He was a soldier.

MARJORIE. And you're just now getting around to divorce papers?

DIERDRE. He's a good man, at heart.

MARJORIE. Seems questionable.

DIERDRE. Point is, no matter what he did to Matthew or Thomas... or Cedric, McKinnon, Martin, James, Liam...Walter...

MARJORIE. *(Interrupting.)* Dierdre!

DIERDRE. He's on his way here now, and...

> *Beau reenters, partially dressed, looking for his clothing.*

…we've got to get out of here, Beau. Or make no mistake, he will kill you!

CLARKE. Good God!

BEAU. I expect he'll be on the next train.

DIERDRE. I expect you're right!

CLARKE. *(With rising hysteria.)* He sounds very volatile!

BEAU. It's me he's after, you lily liver—would you kindly relax!

> *Having found something, but not everything, Beau's off to look in another room.*

CLARKE. Relax??! There's a maniac after my only brother!

MARJORIE. Oh, Clarke, how altruistic.

SYLVIA. *(On an entirely different track.)* I don't get it.

MARJORIE. What?

SYLVIA. *(To Dierdre.)* You're sort of mousy aren't you?

MARJORIE. Sylvie! Don't be rude.

SYLVIA. Well, isn't she? I mean, she's got a husband who's slaughtering soldiers just to keep her his, and a lover who is by far and away the greatest-looking man in Britain.

BEAU. *(Poking back on momentarily.)* Thank you.

> *He's off again.*

CLARKE. Greatest looking? Have you always felt that way?

SYLVIA. To be honest, yes.

CLARKE. That's awful. Why'd you agree to marry me then?

SYLVIA. We were already engaged by the time you introduced me to Beau. And he was already married to Marjorie, and I was already burnt by love anyway, so…

CLARKE. Burnt by love?

SYLVIA. Did you think you were the first man I'd ever been with?

MARJORIE. *(Relishing the moment.)* Ooh, how indelicate, Sylvie.

SYLVIA. You're one to talk! Besides—"the value in virginity is a patriarchal construct," according to our mother-in-law.

BEAU. *(Entering, having found something, but not everything— correcting, with disdain.)* No—that pearl of wisdom can be attributed entirely to Emmeline Pankhurst—Mama's misguided eidolon.

SYLVIA. I'd hardly call the founder of the Women's Social and Political Union "misguided."

> *Sylvia finds his shoe in an unlikely spot and hands it to him.*

CLARKE. *(Still coming to grips.)* So…on our wedding night… you'd already…

SYLVIA. *(Returning to the point.)* Oh dear. Sorry to cloud your day, Clarke. At any rate, here now is Dierdre. A little wisp of a thing, back to my point, and I just don't understand. What's the appeal?

BEAU. She's wonderfully naive, I'd say.

> *He exits again, articles in hand, back to the bedroom.*

SYLVIA. Naive? That's the ticket then?

DIERDRE. Some men tell me it's my titters.

> *Dierdre "titters" her giggle once more.*

CLARKE. I see what they mean.

MARJORIE. Clarke!

SYLVIA. *(Nearly to herself.)* Good Lord, this conversation has gone southward.

CLARKE. I'm just being empathetic.

DIERDRE. You said to be honest.

SYLVIA. No, Marjorie said to be honest.

DIERDRE. Well, you all look alike.

> *A beat. They look to each other.*

SYLVIA. She's enormously pregnant.

MARJORIE. She's wearing a negligee.

CLARKE. And I'm a man!

SYLVIA. We look nothing alike!

DIERDRE. You know what I mean.

SYLVIA. I'm afraid I haven't a clue what any of you mean this morning.

> *Beau appears once more.*

BEAU. *(Finding his pants in an unusual place.)* It seems to me that the best course of action is for the five of us to leave the cottage as soon as possible.

DIERDRE and MARJORIE. Yes!   **CLARKE.** That's what I was
                                            going to say!

SYLVIA. Perhaps I don't want to leave. Perhaps I want Richard to kill you.

CLARKE, MARJORIE, and BEAU. Sylvie!

Dierdre gasps simultaneously.

SYLVIA. What?! I'm a jilted lover, aren't I? Double jilted really, if you count Clarke.

CLARKE. *Count* me? I'm your husband.

SYLVIA. Beau, you've deceived me terribly. Being already married was one thing. But having plans to marry a completely different person, is something else entirely.

MARJORIE. Beau can't marry anyone else, can he? We're still married.

DIERDRE. Are you?

MARJORIE. Indeed.

DIERDRE. But Beau, I thought you said the divorce was final.

MARJORIE. Did you?

BEAU. Final is such an ambiguous word.

DIERDRE. *(To Beau.)* Is that *your* baby then?!

MARJORIE. Oh heavens no. This baby belongs to Sylvia's husband.

DIERDRE. Oh. Well, that's a relief.

SYLVIA. *(Dripping sarcasm.)* Yes. Isn't it?

CLARKE. I think we should gather our things and depart immediately before the brute arrives.

DIERDRE. Yes!

SYLVIA. How are we supposed to depart? We have no car.

MARJORIE. No car?

SYLVIA. We took the train to be discreet.

MARJORIE. How very thoughtful.

DIERDRE. But he'll be coming on the train, won't he? We'll run into him at the station.

BEAU. We'll have to risk it. It's our only escape. Perhaps he won't be violent in public.

DIERDRE. Once he whacked a lovely bloke named Gavin at our local pub.

SYLVIA. You take lovers as often as the queen takes tea.

DIERDRE. *(Paying a compliment.)* You're much more clever than Beau made you out to be.

SYLVIA. *(Livid, to Beau.)* You told her about me?

DIERDRE. Only in that he had a strong-willed sister-in-law.

SYLVIA. Oh, is that what he said?

BEAU. Now, let's not get hung up on semantics.

SYLVIA. Semantics aren't the only thing I'd like to see hung! No thank you. I'm staying put, right here.

> *She sits.*

Let's see what this mass murderer has up his sleeve, thank you very much. My life is worthless now anyway—perhaps he'll redirect his anger at me and I can get this life over with once and for all.

BEAU. Sylvie, please. Be reasonable.

MARJORIE. Yes, Sylvie. Be reasonable.

SYLVIA. I don't believe the two of you are well-suited ambassadors for reason!

BEAU. I've had enough of this! I'm going to pack. Sylvia, I suggest you change.

> *Beau exits back to the bedroom.*

SYLVIA. *(Off to Beau.)* I've done enough changing for today. *(Then to herself.)* Less than an hour ago I was a woman in love on the brink of my life's beginning. Now, I'm on the precipice of divorce with nothing but a killer's entrance to look forward to.

CLARKE. Gah! You're so dramatic!

> *Clarke exits (dramatically) to the kitchen, clearing some-thing perhaps, in preparation to depart.*

SYLVIA. *(Calling after him.)* You're the one who thinks *God* has personally involved himself in your love affair!

MARJORIE. *(Getting her hat, etc.)* I'm sorry you've gotten hold of the wrong end of the stick, Sylvie. But you're still quite pretty really. You'll meet a man eventually. Now gather your things and let's be off.

SYLVIA. I've met men, Marjorie. I even married one…*remember*? I keep trying to convince myself that I'm in love, but the problem is, I was already in love once. I was madly, deeply in love with a boy from Shrewsbury.

MARJORIE. I do *love* a good *love* story, darling. Do you think you might change your clothes, and tell us all about it on the train, where we're not at risk of being slaughtered?

DIERDRE. Oh! That's a good idea!

> *Clarke reenters. Marjorie and Clarke go about gathering their things and readying themselves for departure. (Hats, gloves, umbrella, etc.)*

SYLVIA. William was tall. Taller than your average boy. Broad shouldered. Green eyed.

DIERDRE. My Richard has green eyes.

SYLVIA. Yes, well, your Richard is also a lunatic, and you've divorced him so it's my turn to talk now.

DIERDRE. Right.

SYLVIA. William was gentle.

DIERDRE. Richard is gentle.

SYLVIA. Are you really lamenting your gentle killer of a husband or have I officially lost my mind?!

DIERDRE. He doesn't really act like a killer, you know?

CLARKE. *(Putting a finishing touch on something.)* There we are. Now, Sylvie, if you'd just slip on a proper dress, we can hear all about William on the walk to the train.

SYLVIA. Do what you want Clarke. I'm not leaving. I plan to face this man of mystery head-on.

DIERDRE. He's not particularly mysterious really.

MARJORIE. Why are you defending him?

DIERDRE. I just hate for people to think he's so awful.

CLARKE. And yet, you're quite sure he's en route to kill Beau?

DIERDRE. Quite.

CLARKE. *(Furiously handing Dierdre her hat.)* Shall we?

DIERDRE. *(Lightly.)* Thank you.

SYLVIA. *(Lightbulb.)* You're still in love with your husband, aren't you?!

DIERDRE. Ex-husband and it's not so absolute.

MARJORIE. Well, do you love him or not?

DIERDRE. I don't love Richard in the same way I *love* Beau, but that's not to say I don't love him at all.

SYLVIA. Isn't it all or nothing?

DIERDRE. There's something to be said for loyalty disguised as love.

CLARKE. Is there?

DIERDRE. I never felt about Richard the way I *feel* about Beau.

CLARKE. So, you don't love him?

DIERDRE. Who?

CLARKE. Richard!

DIERDRE. I must have felt enough to marry him, didn't I?

CLARKE. *(At wit's end.)* How should I know?!

DIERDRE. It's only now that I've uncovered this new, magnified version of love with Beau, that I realize the love I thought was love with Richard, was merely an allegiance.

CLARKE. An allegiance?

DIERDRE. A safety.

MARJORIE. With a murderer?!

DIERDRE. I didn't know he was a murderer when I married him.

CLARKE. *(Furiously handing Dierdre her gloves.)* Look at the time!

DIERDRE. *(Lightly.)* Thank you.

SYLVIA. So what are you saying? You're operating on a ladderlike system of love?

DIERDRE. What a clever way to put it. Yes, I suppose I am.

SYLVIA. So you propose there are varying degrees of love? Like on a thermometer?

DIERDRE. Ha! Yes! That's it precisely!

SYLVIA. Huh. Finally, you've said something I can understand.

MARJORIE. I've no idea what she's talking about. Let's go!

CLARKE. *(With genuine curiosity.)* Where am I on your thermometer, Sylvie?

MARJORIE. What difference does that make, Clarke?

CLARKE. Just curious is all.

SYLVIA. Ha! I suddenly feel lighter! I feel like dancing.

DIERDRE. I knew this was a party!

SYLVIA. Dance with me!

> *Sylvia turns the music on. She and Dierdre begin to dance. Gradually, Clarke gets into the dancing as well.*

MARJORIE. Clarke, do you know what happens when one loses one's mind? Would one start dancing out of the blue?

CLARKE. It's possible.

MARJORIE. Well do something!

CLARKE. Sylvia—

SYLVIA. You're no husband of mine. Why should I do your bidding?

CLARKE. We may not have had a lasting marriage, but that doesn't mean I want to see you killed.

SYLVIA. How generous of you. But now, I think I'll stay right here and think of my sweet William.

DIERDRE. Then I will too!

SYLVIA. *(From a dip in Dierdre's arms, up to heaven.)* I wonder if he's looking down on us right now.

DIERDRE. Oh, I hope so! Why didn't you marry him?

MARJORIE. This is preposterous! Dierdre, please don't encourage her.

> *Marjorie turns off the music. Sylvia, Dierdre, and Clarke stop dancing.*

SYLVIA. Good old Marjorie. Always up to spoil a laugh.

MARJORIE. I'm just trying to avoid a murder scene!

DIERDRE. *(Back on target.)* Oh yes!

SYLVIA. *(To Dierdre.)* We wanted to marry, Dierdre, but he joined the Navy and was killed in the war.

DIERDRE. *(Easily distracted.)* Oh no!

SYLVIA. I was seventeen. William had a job in my father's apothecary. Stocking shelves, sweeping up, you know. After school I would manage the till. We would make eyes at one another across the aisles. It was incredibly romantic.

MARJORIE. Yes, drugstores are famous for their dim lighting. Sylvie, please get dressed!

SYLVIA. My father would leave the store and William and I would share toffees and sticky kisses when the customers had gone.

DIERDRE. That does sound romantic.

CLARKE. So he joined the Navy, and that was that, now go get dressed.

SYLVIA. The morning of his funeral my heart died. The man I knew I was meant to love was no more, and therefore I knew nothing else would ever really matter.

CLARKE. Nothing?

DIERDRE. *(Choked up.)* Oh, you poor, poor girl.

SYLVIA. And then my father met Clarke's father at a pharmaceuticals assembly, and the rest, as they say, was history.

CLARKE. How come you never told me about this? About William?

MARJORIE. What do you care, Clarke?

CLARKE. It's just information I would've liked to have had!

SYLVIA. Really, Clarke. You might not love me at the moment, but there was a time when you were quite fond of me. I doubt you'd wanted to hear about my past lover.

CLARKE. I expect you're right. Only now for you to say that nothing after him mattered, implies that I never mattered. That's a bit of a blow, isn't it?

SYLVIA. I'd say in light of your present behavior, it's neither here nor there.

MARJORIE. Hear, hear! Now, Sylvie, won't you please get dressed?!! It really would be frightful to leave you here alone.

DIERDRE. Oh yes! It truly would. Despite the fact that he really is a nice fellow, Richard is a madman.

> *Beau enters with his luggage, dressed handsomely, without his shoes, his tie untied.*

BEAU. Right then, let's be off. *(Noticing.)* Sylvie, you're not dressed.

SYLVIA. Oh, you're all incorrigible! Fine, give me a moment.

BEAU. Well, hurry please. The next train leaves on the hour—and it's at least a ten-minute walk.

SYLVIA. I'll be quick, Beau. Like your heart.

> *Sylvia exits to the bedroom.*

DIERDRE. All that dancing! I think I'll have some water. Anyone else?

MARJORIE. No, thank you.   **BEAU.** Not I.   **CLARKE.** Scotch for me.

> *Dierdre exits to the kitchen. Clarke fixes himself a drink at the bar.*

BEAU. *(Re: his tie.)* Darling, you know I'm useless. Do you mind?

MARJORIE. Alright, quickly then.

> *She ties his tie throughout.*

Are you angry with us?

BEAU. What right have I to be angry?

MARJORIE. I'm a bit miffed, I must admit.

BEAU. Are you?

MARJORIE. I'd never have strayed, had you been faithful.

BEAU. You knew?

MARJORIE. Well, of course, darling. The wife always knows.

BEAU. Why didn't you say anything?

MARJORIE. I hate unpleasant conversation.

CLARKE. She really does. One time I mentioned—

49

MARJORIE. *(Interrupting—sternly.)* Clarke.

CLARKE. *(Saving face.)* Nothing! I mentioned nothing!

MARJORIE. I think I loved you terribly when we first met.

BEAU. Did you?

MARJORIE. Didn't you love me?

BEAU. I thought we made a handsome couple.

MARJORIE. Is that love?

BEAU. I was fine.

MARJORIE. Is fine enough for you?

BEAU. I've always thought so.

MARJORIE. Well, I don't want to be someone else's "fine."

BEAU. That's understandable.

MARJORIE. Thank you.

CLARKE. *(Popping up between them.)* I hope you'll come to the wedding.

BEAU. Wedding?

MARJORIE. Yes, Beau. I'm hoping we can be sharp about a divorce. I'd like to be properly wed to Clarke by the time the baby comes.

BEAU. Not so scandalous after all then, divorce?

MARJORIE. What choice do I have, really?

CLARKE. Fortunately, she won't have to change her name.

> *The tie is tied. Dierdre pokes her head out of the kitchen door.*

DIERDRE. Anyone want a picnic for the road?

> *All at once...*

MARJORIE. Yes, please. **BEAU.** Why not? **CLARKE.** Lovely.

DIERDRE. Right.

> *Dierdre disappears back into the kitchen.*

MARJORIE. Will you do it, Beau? Will you draw up the papers?

BEAU. You're certain then, that Clarke is the husband for you?

MARJORIE. I am.

BEAU. All this certainty is a bit unnerving.

MARJORIE. How so?

Beau shines/laces his shoes throughout the following.

BEAU. Well, you see, I'm not a bit certain there's a precisely perfect woman for me.

MARJORIE. Why not?

BEAU. There's so many of them. Certainty seems an impossible task.

MARJORIE. *(With eyes for Clarke.)* When you're in love, you'll know.

BEAU. But that's just it.

MARJORIE. What?

BEAU. I must have been in love.

MARJORIE. With me?

BEAU. But by your theory, it would seem that I haven't.

MARJORIE. I never said…

BEAU. By your philosophy, in fact, I have not yet found the correct person to be in love with.

MARJORIE. Well…

BEAU. Thus proving that actually, I've never been in love. So then, if that's true, I ask, what if the right woman for me is on the other side of the earth entirely?

CLARKE. In Antarctica!

BEAU. Precisely. What if I never meet her because she's too busy doing whatever it is she's doing in Antarctica?

CLARKE. *(A genuine question.)* What *do* women do in Antarctica?

DIERDRE. *(From the front door—holding a bouquet of flowers.)* Alright to bring some flowers from the garden back to town?

ALL. Lovely.

DIERDRE. Right.

She shuts the door.

MARJORIE. That's an awfully odd way to think about things.

BEAU. It's quite logical actually. If every person waited to marry until a moment of absolute certitude, than I suspect there would be very few marriages altogether.

MARJORIE. Your pragmatism is becoming pessimistic.

BEAU. Marrying for the assuredness of love, is uncommon at best.

MARJORIE. I don't think so!

BEAU. Well, I do. But—are the bonds of matrimony therefore so easily dismissed?

MARJORIE. Well—if the married people are unhappy…

BEAU. No. I say marriage is a choice and therefore must be adhered to by its participants.

His shoes are tied.

CLARKE. *(A brotherly dig.)* Quoth the man from the cottage with his wife and two lovers.

DIERDRE. *(Popping up within the window seat.)* Ha! Did you know there's a secret passage from the garden shed?

ALL. *(Ad-libbed.)* Yes, yes, we know. *(Etc.)*

DIERDRE. Right.

She shuts the lid back on herself.

BEAU. It was never my intent to divorce you, Marji. Living as we were, husband and wife, that was a commitment I intended to keep.

MARJORIE. Aside from faithfulness?

BEAU. In my opinion, faithfulness is an entirely separate matter from marriage.

MARJORIE. How can you say that? They're entirely dependent upon each other.

BEAU. I'd venture to guess some of the most lasting marriages, when uncovered, were not at all faithful ones.

MARJORIE. But you think they were happy nonetheless?

BEAU. I find that question irrelevant to the issue.

MARJORIE. *(Fed up.)* Please let's stop this ridiculous banter. The merits of fidelity aside, the point I make to you, dear husband, is that I am not interested in an unhappy, faithless marriage any longer!

CLARKE. Nor am I!

BEAU. *(Accepting defeat.)* Right then. *(Saving face.)* Well, I'm a barrister, aren't I? I can have those papers drawn immediately.

MARJORIE. Thank you.

Beau is dressed, packed, and ready to go.

BEAU. That is, if I'm not killed today.

CLARKE. *(To Marjorie.)* What will we do then?

MARJORIE. Well, he'd be dead, so I'd be free to marry anyway.

CLARKE. Right you are.

BEAU. *(Sarcastic.)* Lovely.

Beau moves to the bedroom door.

Sylvia, please hurry, I'm ready.

SYLVIA. *(From off.)* Bug off!

BEAU. *(Forcibly squelching his ire.)* Splendid.

MARJORIE. Have another drink it will calm your nerves. Scotch?

CLARKE. Make that two.

DIERDRE. *(Popping in from the kitchen.)* Beau darling, would you like me to bring these little chocolates with the jelly inside?

BEAU. Lovely.

DIERDRE. God, you're handsome.

She kisses him, then pops out again.

MARJORIE. *(As she fixes drinks, quietly.)* Beau? Are you in love, according to your terms, with *Dierdre*?

BEAU. I find her refreshing.

CLARKE. I can see that.

MARJORIE. Not too clearly, I hope.

CLARKE. Not at all, darling.

BEAU. She's lighter than air. She lifts my spirit. She thinks only of me.

MARJORIE. She makes you happy?

BEAU. She's a good distraction.

MARJORIE. I wasn't aware you required distraction.

CLARKE. Do you think her husband is really murderous?

MARJORIE. Why would she say so otherwise?

Dierdre enters holding picnic baskets for the train.

DIERDRE. Say what?

Sylvia enters dressed beautifully.

SYLVIA. Ready.

DIERDRE. You look lovely!

BEAU. Finally. Let's be gone then. Lights out.

They ad-lib, simultaneously, as they ready themselves to depart:

SYLVIA. Have you got everything you need? *(Etc.)*

BEAU. Did you turn the lights off upstairs? *(Etc.)*

CLARKE. Darling, would you like to use the privy one more time before we go? *(Etc.)*

MARJORIE. I'm not looking forward to another train ride, I barely fit in the compartment. *(Etc.)*

DIERDRE. I wish we had binoculars so we could see him coming. *(Etc.)*

They go about putting out cigarettes, finishing drinks, gathering suitcases, and turning off lights. Dierdre is once more overloaded with her baggage and now baskets of food.

As they all weave in and out of line, getting themselves into position to leave the house, their ad-lib evolves into a series of:

ALL. *(Freely, on top of each other.)* Pardon me./Excuse me./Sorry.

Until finally...

BEAU. Ready?

ALL. Ready.

They approach the front door.

A deliberate knock at the door is heard.

All at once, they gasp, drop their luggage, and look out.

Another knock is heard.

DIERDRE. *(Whispered, brilliant realization.)* I think it's Richard!

MARJORIE. *(Whispered, biting sarcasm.)* Yes, thank you, dear.

CLARKE. What should we do?

SYLVIA. I'm going to open the door.

CLARKE, MARJORIE, DIERDRE, and BEAU. What?!

SYLVIA. It's the anticipation that's worse than the reality, isn't that right, Clarke?

CLARKE. There wasn't a murderer on the other side of the door when I said that, Sylvie!

DIERDRE. I'm afraid you don't understand what Richard's capable of!

Faster, deliberate knocking.

SYLVIA. I am going to open that door. If you do not want to be here when I do, I suggest you hide.

DIERDRE. Brilliant! Let's hide!

They all (except Sylvia) idiotically seek hiding spots. Behind a potted plant, under an umbrella, in the window nook, under the sofa, etc. They ad-lib freely and simultaneously:

BEAU. Yes, I'll take my old hide-and-find spot from when I was a boy. No one ever found me there. (Etc.)

CLARKE. I know the perfect hiding spot, when I was a child I fit perfectly. (Etc.)

MARJORIE. I've got a baby to think about! I'm too young to die! (Etc.)

DIERDRE. Everyone is taking all the good spots! Where shall I go?! Where shall I go?! (Etc.)

Then, over the knocking, now taking control.

SYLVIA. Oh, for heaven's sake. Clarke, take your pregnant sister-in-law up to the bedroom. Beau, you and your *morning surprise* can retreat into the guest suite.* I shall let you all know when it's safe.

They all begin to exit accordingly. More knocking.

DIERDRE. My you're brave.

MARJORIE. Don't mistake bravery for martyrdom, darling.

CLARKE. But how will we know if he hurts you?

SYLVIA. I'll try to scream appropriately. Now off you go.

BEAU. (Heroically.) Sylvia… (Cowardly.) Be careful.

---

* Destinations can be determined by staging. Lines can be altered accordingly.

He's off.

SYLVIA. You should have said that seven years ago.

More knocking.

Beau, Dierdre, Clarke, and Marjorie are gone. Sylvia stands alone facing the door. She takes a breath. She opens the door. Wind blows, birds chirp. Richard, pointing an enormous gun in Sylvia's face, enters the cottage. Sylvia gasps, stands back, and then notices…

William?

Blackout.

End of Act One

ACT TWO

Lights rise on the same tableau as the end of Act One. Richard stands in the foyer, gun pointed at Sylvia. The door is still open. Wind blows, birds chirp. It's the shock of their lives.

SYLVIA. William?

RICHARD. *(Lowers his gun and drops his murderous disposition.)* Sylvia?

> *Richard slams the door shut.*
>
> *Sylvia screams!*
>
> *Everyone else in the house screams!*
>
> *Richard screams! He aims his gun every which way.*
>
> *The dialogue between Richard and Sylvia should be kept as secretive as possible to prevent the others from overhearing.*

SYLVIA. But you're dead!

RICHARD. Is it really you?

SYLVIA. I could ask the same of you!

RICHARD. You look beautiful.

CLARKE. *(Calling from off.)* Be warned you criminal, I'm calling the constable!

> *Richard rearms himself. Sylvia swiftly moves back and forth between the bottom of the staircase and Richard.*

SYLVIA. *(Calling off.)* No Clarke, don't!

CLARKE. *(Calling from off.)* Don't?

SYLVIA. *(Calling off.)* Please don't!

CLARKE. *(Calling from off.)* You screamed!

SYLVIA. *(Whispered to Richard.)* Are you going to kill me?

RICHARD. *(Whispered.)* Heavens no!

SYLVIA. *(Calling off.)* I'm fine!

CLARKE. *(Calling from off.)* Fine?

RICHARD. *(Whispered.)* Who's that?

SYLVIA. *(Whispered.)* My husband.

RICHARD. *(Whispered.)* I see.

CLARKE. *(Calling from off.)* I'm coming down!

SYLVIA. *(Calling off.)* No! No Clarke! Not yet. I'll let you know!

CLARKE. *(Calling from off.)* Well alright then, Sylvie, but let this be a warning!…

    Beat.

SYLVIA. *(Calling off.)* Is that it dear? Was that the warning?

CLARKE. *(Calling from off.)* Right then.

    Their dialogue continues hushed.

RICHARD. Is your husband *hiding* upstairs?

SYLVIA. Well, now you know he's there so I suppose he's done a poor job of it—can this be true? William Pierce? I was only just now talking of you! It's as if the universe heard me.

RICHARD. How grand!

SYLVIA. I thought I'd lost you forever!

RICHARD. And I you.

SYLVIA. How'd you find me?

RICHARD. I didn't.

SYLVIA. What?

RICHARD. I mean I'm not looking for you.

SYLVIA. But you've found me.

RICHARD. Thank God!

SYLVIA. Well if you're not here to find me, whatever are you doing here?

RICHARD. *(Remembering his mission—returning to his hunt.)* My wife has left me for another man and I've come to find him.

SYLVIA. *(Not hushed.)* You're Richard!

RICHARD. *(A gentle confession.)* It's my pseudonym.

    He's back to the hunt.

SYLVIA. You're married to Dierdre!

RICHARD. *(Genuine surprise.)* You know her?

SYLVIA. Yes.

RICHARD. *(Pathetically emotional, despite unconsciously pointing the gun toward Sylvia.)* She's decided to leave me.

SYLVIA. Would you mind terribly putting your gun down while we determine why any woman would decide to leave you?

RICHARD. *(Politely.)* Oh! Sorry. Of course.

> *He sets his gun down.*

SYLVIA. There now. A breath of relief.

> *They breathe in unison. Dialogue resumes hushed.*

RICHARD. This is a lovely cottage.

SYLVIA. It belongs to my mother-in-law.

RICHARD. *(Sincere.)* I didn't mean to frighten you, Sylvie. Lord knows, in a million years, I never thought I'd find you here. God. You look ravishing.

SYLVIA. *(Flattered.)* Thanks. *(Back on task.)* But, that's quite besides the point. *(With joy.)* William, you're alive?!

RICHARD. I am!

SYLVIA. *(With despair.)* But your wife says…

RICHARD. *(Interrupting.)* Ex-wife.

SYLVIA. Most people do choose to divorce murderers, darling.

RICHARD. *(Confused.)* Murderers?

SYLVIA. I never would have thought it, William. You were always gentle as a lamb.

RICHARD. *(Hurt.)* But you can't think I've actually killed anyone?

SYLVIA. Haven't you?

RICHARD. *(Offended.)* Sylvie!

SYLVIA. Dierdre says there's a bloke buried in your back porch steps!

RICHARD. *(A realization.)* She really is gullible isn't she?

SYLVIA. And Gavin at the local pub?

RICHARD. *(A decision to explain.)* My ex-wife is a bit of a free spirit, Sylvia. I thought—

SYLVIA. What?

RICHARD. *(Not quite finding the words.)* Well, I thought—

SYLVIA. Yes?

RICHARD. *(Ashamed.)* I made up stories to frighten her into staying with me.

SYLVIA. You fabricated murders?

RICHARD. *(Apologetically.)* Wellll…

SYLVIA. But you're here, aren't you? With a rather large gun, I might add.

RICHARD. *(Matter-of-fact.)* It's not loaded.

SYLVIA. So, you're not a murderer?

RICHARD. *(With pride.)* I'm a fantastic storyteller.

SYLVIA. You always did have a way with words.

RICHARD. *(Humbly.)* I'm thinking of becoming a writer.

CLARKE. *(Calling from off.)* Sylvia?!

SYLVIA. *(Calling up the stairs.)* Still fine, Clarke!

CLARKE. *(Calling from off.)* Just checking.

SYLVIA. *(Calling off.)* Right darling.

> *Sylvia returns to Richard.*

RICHARD. He seems nice.

SYLVIA. Bit of a philanderer.

RICHARD. Ah.

SYLVIA. My mind is all in a jumble.

RICHARD. It's wonderful to see you, Sylvia.

SYLVIA. What were you going to do with that gun then?

RICHARD. Hm? *(Remembering his mission.)* Oh. Scare the fellow.

SYLVIA. Beau Van Kipness?

RICHARD. *(Surprised once more.)* You know him?

SYLVIA. Indeed.

RICHARD. *(Back to the hunt.)* Is he here?

SYLVIA. He is.

RICHARD. *(Curious.)* Where?

SYLVIA. Hiding.

RICHARD. *(Impressed.)* Successfully.

SYLVIA. I suppose so.

RICHARD. *(Bravely.)* Coward.

SYLVIA. Quite.

RICHARD. *(Back to a fool in love.)* You're looking so lovely.

SYLVIA. Your eyes haven't changed a bit. Warm. Gentle.

RICHARD. I've dreamt of this moment. *(Re: the gun.)* Well, not this moment exactly…but—seeing you again.

SYLVIA. I always thought it unsettling that your body wasn't found. All these years I've mourned you. You've got a tombstone. Your parents think you're dead. All of Shrewsbury thinks you're dead.

RICHARD. How are my parents?

SYLVIA. Dead!

RICHARD. How awful.

SYLVIA. Oh, William.

RICHARD. Oh, Sylvia.

SYLVIA. How I've longed for you.

RICHARD. And I you.

> *They rush to each other. In their haste, Richard's gun drops to the ground. It goes off with a very loud bang.*
>
> *They scream, and screams are heard throughout the house. (Perhaps the bullet strikes a china figurine, or some such object, creating a Rube Goldberg–ricochet effect.)*

SYLVIA. I thought you said it wasn't loaded!

RICHARD. I thought it wasn't! I've never been good with guns! Perhaps it was slightly loaded.

SYLVIA. That leads to slightly dead doesn't it?

> *Richard takes the gun, clearly not an expert, and examines it.*

RICHARD. It's empty now. For certain.

SYLVIA. Let me see it.

> *She expertly examines the gun.*

Gate. Cylinder. Chamber. Hammer. *(Then.)* Right. Good then.

Sylvia sets the gun down.

Beau enters with a makeshift weapon (fire poker, taxidermized animal, etc.) drawn, en garde! A standoff!

BEAU. Aha! I am Beau Van Kipness! It's me you're after! Let the girl go!

SYLVIA. *(Flattered.)* Beau! How noble!

BEAU. Step aside, Sylvie, you're free now!

SYLVIA. Thank you, Beau, but I'm fine. Really. Will you excuse us?

BEAU. Pardon?

SYLVIA. Go back to the bedroom, darling. I'm quite fine.

BEAU. I heard a gunshot.

SYLVIA. Indeed you did.

BEAU. *(As though rehearsed.)* This is my home! No one opens fire in my home!

SYLVIA. Right, well, we'll keep that in mind, darling. Now, beg your pardon, off you go.

BEAU. Sylvie, I can't leave you with a murderer!

SYLVIA. Oh? Now you've decided to qualify *how* you'll leave me?

BEAU. *(Pulling her aside.)* Sylvie, I am sorry about Dierdre. About everything. And now, thinking of you in danger, I… Well, I think, perhaps I really do love you.

SYLVIA. That's all I've ever wanted you to say and now that fear of my death has caused you to say it, it's the very last thing I want to hear. Perhaps I do believe you Beau, but you see, it's no matter, because I'm quite sure I'm only partially on your thermometer.

BEAU. What?

SYLVIA. Please leave us for the time being.

BEAU. *(Back en garde.)* Leave you with this killer?

SYLVIA. None of us are free of sin.

BEAU. *(An attempt at authority.)* But Sylvia!

SYLVIA. *(A better attempt than his.)* Beau!

BEAU. Right then. Excuse me.

Beau exits (perhaps backing up, still en garde). Once he's gone...

RICHARD. So that was him?

SYLVIA. Yes.

RICHARD. That was brave of him.

SYLVIA. He's not all bad.

RICHARD. Why didn't you tell him?

SYLVIA. Tell him what?

RICHARD. Who I am.

SYLVIA. It's been a morning of spilled secrets. I'd rather like to keep this one to myself for a while.

They resume their romantic posture.

RICHARD. I can't believe I'm looking at you.

SYLVIA. I barely recognized you.

RICHARD. I've aged haven't I? Put on a few.

SYLVIA. No matter. It's you, isn't it?

RICHARD. It is.

SYLVIA. Your beard suits you, William.

RICHARD. *(Slowly, a confession.)* It's not mine.

SYLVIA. No?

Richard removes his beard.

Oh!

RICHARD. Things aren't always what they seem.

SYLVIA. No?

Richard removes his mustache.

Oh!

RICHARD. I can't say I'm proud.

SYLVIA. No?

Richard removes his hat/fake hair. Perhaps he's bald.

Oh.

Beat.

William—please. Tell me the truth.

RICHARD. I left the Navy.

SYLVIA. Without dying?

RICHARD. I was…discharged.

SYLVIA. Honorably I hope.

Richard shakes his head slowly, no.

Oh no. *(Then.)* Assault?

He shakes his head no.

Treason?!

He shakes his head no.

Espionage?!!

RICHARD. *(A desperate confession.)* I was cold! All the time! The blankets were uncomfortable and I had terrible blisters. I was miserable, Sylvia. And…and…I missed you.

SYLVIA. Oh, William.

RICHARD. For two years, I'd been stationed at Rosyth in Scotland in readiness to stop any large-scale breakout attempt by the Germans.

SYLVIA. My hero!

RICHARD. My commanding officer was having me transferred to Scapa Flow in the Orkneys.

SYLVIA. How decidedly foreign.

RICHARD. He gave me a weekend leave between deployments.

SYLVIA. Generous.

RICHARD. *(Skirting the issue.)* Rather.

SYLVIA. *(Putting two and two together.)* Ah. So you never made it to the Orkneys?

RICHARD. *(The admission.)* Never did.

SYLVIA. *(With total understanding.)* Huh.

RICHARD. I couldn't take it anymore. When I got to London, I burned my uniform, rented a one-room flat with the money I'd saved working for your father, and hid out for a while.

SYLVIA. You poor dear.

RICHARD. It was a dark time, Sylvia. I waited out the war. Two long years I lived like a hermit, picking up odd jobs at the shipyards. Finally, when the war ended, I found my courage. And the way back to your parents' house.

SYLVIA. But I was married by then.

RICHARD. Yes.

SYLVIA. Tragic!

RICHARD. I hid in the bushes outside your parents' home.

SYLVIA. Romantic!

RICHARD. I saw you, you know? You'd come for dinner with your husband. And so I knew I was too late.

SYLVIA. But, William, why didn't you say something?

RICHARD. You were married, Sylvia. I'd lost you forever. And I was forever a traitor. There was no use.

SYLVIA. So you bought a beard and changed your name to Richard?

RICHARD. It was an impossible situation, Sylvie. Stay myself, and risk a lifetime of shame, or reinvent myself, and start anew.

SYLVIA. There is something refreshing about starting anew.

RICHARD. I thought so.

SYLVIA. You know, I thought I was starting anew this morning.

RICHARD. Did you?

SYLVIA. But it all went dreadfully wrong.

RICHARD. I'm sorry to hear that.

SYLVIA. Don't be! Now you're here and I…I…

>   *It has become too intimate.*

I could do with a cup of tea. You?

RICHARD. Certainly. Thank you.

SYLVIA. Make yourself at home, William. I'll be right back.

>   *Sylvia exits to the kitchen. Church bells begin to ring to claim the hour. Ten A.M. As the distant bells ring, Sylvia pops her head back in.*

Crumpets, William?

RICHARD. Yes, please.

SYLVIA. Lovely.

> *She disappears again. He takes in the room. Perhaps looks out the window.*

> *He takes off his murderous outer coat to reveal an outfit fitting a pharmacist. He puts on a pair of sweet glasses. He smooths his hair.*

> *Though no longer a criminal, he is not the handsome devil that Beau is, nor the crisp-suited chap that Clarke is; William looks decidedly kind. Sylvia reenters with tea and crumpets.*

Who would have thought when I woke up this morning that I'd be serving tea to my once betrothed, dead, now alive, William Pierce from Shrewsbury? One lump or two?

> *Sylvia puts sugar cubes in his teacup.*

RICHARD. None, thank you.

> *She quickly removes the sugar cubes from his teacup and puts them back—now wet—in the sugar bowl.*

SYLVIA. Of course. Sorry. It's been so long.

> *Sylvia hands him the tea, sans sugar.*

RICHARD. And yet it's as if no time has passed at all.

SYLVIA. I'm glad you feel that way.

RICHARD. I opened my own apothecary, you know?

SYLVIA. How could I know anything?

RICHARD. Right after I met Dierdre.

SYLVIA. A little wisp of a thing, isn't she?

RICHARD. She's a good distraction. If I couldn't have (you)…

> *At the word "distraction," Clarke bounds down the stairs (perhaps he trips and falls) screaming loudly, holding a large vase above his head poised for attack.*

CLARKE. Unhand her, you beast!

RICHARD. Who's this?

SYLVIA. Clarke!

CLARKE. This is my wife, you scoundrel! You let her free!

SYLVIA. *(Helping him up.)* Clarke! Oh my, dear Clarke. Aren't you the knight in shining armor? Darling, I'm quite alright.

CLARKE. But I heard a gunshot.

SYLVIA. That was ages ago.

CLARKE. Yes, well, it took me some time to determine a proper weapon and come up with a plan.

SYLVIA. The vase and the screaming were quite well thought out, darling.

> *Beau enters, another makeshift weapon drawn.*

BEAU. What's going on?

SYLVIA. *(Exasperated.)* Nothing!

CLARKE. *(To Sylvia.)* How can you be so nonchalant?

BEAU. *(Subtly to Richard.)* You look different.

SYLVIA. *(Carrying on.)* I'm fine. Both of you. We—well, we just need a bit more time to sort things out—don't we Wi…Richard?

RICHARD. *(Sipping tea—pinkies up.)* Mm, yes. Yes, we do.

CLARKE. *(As if rehearsed.)* Well, this is my home. No one opens fire in my home!

BEAU. That's what I said!

CLARKE. Yes, well I'm saying it now!

SYLVIA. Beau, please! We've been through this.

BEAU. *(An attempt at authority.)* Sylvia.

SYLVIA. *(A better attempt than his.)* Beau.

BEAU. Right. Excuse me.

> *Beau exits, backing up once again (perhaps still en garde).*
> *Once he's gone…*

CLARKE. Sylvia?

SYLVIA. Clarke. I'm fine. Now off you go.

CLARKE. Off I go? But Sylvia, you're my wife! I can't leave you with a murderer.

SYLVIA. To what do I owe this sudden spurt of caring?

CLARKE. I don't know really. *(A lightbulb.)* Oh dear.

SYLVIA. What?

CLARKE. Perhaps I still love you?!

SYLVIA. Funny how the brink of death brings out the sentimental side in men. Clarke, please don't confuse the issue. I may be your wife, but you've made it perfectly clear that you do not love me.

CLARKE. I never...

SYLVIA. I believe Marjorie's belly screamed it quite clearly.

CLARKE. Sylvia... *(To Richard politely.)* May I have a word?

RICHARD. Of course. Pardon me, I'll refresh the tea.

> *Richard exits to the kitchen, perhaps stepping deliberately over the gun while gazing lovingly at Sylvia.*

CLARKE. *(Appalled.)* Are you having tea with him?!

SYLVIA. Yes, darling.

RICHARD. *(Popping his head back in.)* Forgive me. Sir, would *you* care for tea?

CLARKE. *(Politely.)* No. Thank you.

> *Richard pops out again.*

SYLVIA. What is it you wanted to say, Clarke?

CLARKE. *(Terribly confused.)* I don't know exactly. Only, it all seems so odd.

SYLVIA. I couldn't agree more.

CLARKE. He seems quite gentlemanly for a killer.

SYLVIA. All of us are capable of hiding secrets.

CLARKE. Sylvia, I did love you. At one time I loved you very much. Perhaps we've just grown weary of one another.

SYLVIA. But that's just it, Clarke. True love is not wearisome. We matched ourselves well, I suppose. But ours was not a romance. *(A realization.)* Oh!

CLARKE. *(On high alert!)* What is it?

SYLVIA. *(Carrying on.)* I'm not the first to utter those words today.

CLARKE. No?

SYLVIA. Beau said the same to me earlier, only I was too wrapped up in pretend to really notice it.

CLARKE. I'm not sure I follow.

SYLVIA. No matter. Our marriage was lovely Clarke, but it wasn't to be.

CLARKE. No, I suppose not.

SYLVIA. Well don't look so glum. You've got your God-chosen Marjorie, haven't you?

CLARKE. Quite right. Quite right.

SYLVIA. *(Comforting.)* Alright then. Up you go. I want to finish my conversation with…Richard.

CLARKE. You're sure you're not in danger?

SYLVIA. Quite.

CLARKE. Up I go then.

> *Clarke moves to exit up the stairs. Just as he hits the top landing…*

SYLVIA. Clarke?

CLARKE. Mm?

SYLVIA. Thank you.

CLARKE. For what?

SYLVIA. For loving me on some level.

CLARKE. Right.

> *Clarke exits. Sylvia opens the kitchen door.*
>
> *Dierdre begins to creep or even crawl on, unnoticed by the others.*

SYLVIA. *(Calling off to Richard.)* All's clear. You can come out.

RICHARD. Whose home is this?

SYLVIA. They're brothers.

RICHARD. Fascinating.

> *Dierdre has picked up the gun and is now aiming it at Richard.*

DIERDRE. *(As menacing as Dierdre gets.)* Hello, Richard!

SYLVIA. Dierdre!

RICHARD. Darling!

DIERDRE. I'm not your darling! And I'm not married to you anymore! All you do is kill the people I love. Well, no more! I love Beau (!)—and Beau loves me (!)—and we're to be married and I won't let you stop me! The stars have aligned! Sylvia, step aside!

Sylvia steps aside.

RICHARD. What do you know of stars?

DIERDRE. I know when they're aligned!

RICHARD. Are you going to kill me?

DIERDRE. I'd sooner kill you than have you kill Beau!

SYLVIA. But what about loyalty?

DIERDRE. *(A quote she's heard.)* "Sometimes we must kill one love to make room for another."

SYLVIA. That's twice now you've made sense.

RICHARD. Has our life together meant nothing to you?

DIERDRE. *(Momentarily thoughtful.)* I don't want to hurt your feelings.

RICHARD. Yet you're pointing a rifle at me.

DIERDRE. *(Letting it all out.)* Fine then! You stifle me! Cooped up all day and night in that dreadful drugstore. At least before I married you, I was free to do as I please.

RICHARD. Before you married me you were living in squalor.

DIERDRE. That's besides the point! I won't let you kill Beau!

With a scream, she shoots! Nothing happens.

RICHARD. I can't believe you'd really kill me!

DIERDRE. *(Befuddled, shaking the gun, staring down the barrel, etc.)* What's happened?

SYLVIA. It's not loaded.

DIERDRE. But I heard a gunshot before!

SYLVIA. It was only *slightly* loaded.

DIERDRE. Oh dear!

CLARKE. *(Calling from off.)* Sylvia?!

SYLVIA. *(Calling up.)* Yes, Clarke?

CLARKE. *(Calling from off.)* I heard a scream.

70

SYLVIA. *(Calling up.)* That was Dierdre.

CLARKE. *(Calling from off.)* Alrighty then…

RICHARD. Dierdre, I wasn't ever going to kill Beau.

DIERDRE. Ha! You've killed all the others!

RICHARD. No!

DIERDRE. No?!

RICHARD. I haven't hurt a flea.

DIERDRE. You said you did!

RICHARD. I only meant to keep you from straying.

DIERDRE. What are you saying?

RICHARD. You have me all wrong. I made up those awful stories to deter you from leaving me. I have a fear of loneliness I'm afraid.

DIERDRE. Is this a joke? I've been living in constant fear of you.

RICHARD. And I of you. I couldn't bear it if you'd left me. I couldn't manage the pain twice. You see, I'd already lost…

DIERDRE. *(Impatient.)* You'd already lost what??!

> *The telephone interrupts.*

SYLVIA. *(To Richard and Dierdre.)* Hold that thought.

> *Richard and Dierdre ad-lib. ("Oh, of course." "Yes." "By all means." Etc.) They immediately set their intense argument temporarily aside, sit, and turn full attention to Sylvia; she answers the phone.*

Van Kipness residence.

This is Mrs. Sylvia Van Kipness, yes.

Oh! Oh my. When?

Yes, of course. I understand.

No, I'll tell them. Thank you.

> *Sylvia hangs up the phone. Richard and Dierdre resume their intense previous position.*

DIERDRE. *(Right back to it.)* What? Richard, what had you lost?

SYLVIA. *(Calling off.)* Beau? I'm afraid I have some news. Can you come out here please? *Beau?*

> *Sylvia moves to shout for Beau, then Clarke, then Marjorie.*

71

There is a certain tempo to the quick succession of name-calling.

DIERDRE. *Richard!*

SYLVIA. *Clarke?*

RICHARD. *Dierdre!*

SYLVIA. *Marjorie?*

RICHARD. *Sylvia!*

SYLVIA. Can you all please come out now? I've had a call.

DIERDRE. Richard?! I demand to know.

SYLVIA. Dierdre, what difference does it make? The point is, he is not here to kill Beau.

> *Beau, with another makeshift weapon, and Clarke, with his own makeshift weapon (a golf club, an umbrella, etc.), cautiously enter, weapons drawn, just in time to hear the end of Sylvia's line. Dierdre stands, gun still in hand.*

BEAU. *(Putting down his weapon.)* Well that's happy news.

SYLVIA. Where's Marjorie?

CLARKE. Is it safe for her, Sylvie? What's going on?

SYLVIA. Quite safe, Clarke, I assure you.

DIERDRE. What's going on is my Richard may or may not be a murderer, but he is most definitely a liar! Ooooh, I'm so mad I could kill you!

> *Dierdre, in one fell swoop, lands atop Richard on the sofa, strangling him dramatically.*

CLARKE. Not quite out of the woods yet, are we?

SYLVIA. The gun is not loaded.

DIERDRE. No, it isn't! *(Shooting the empty gun repeatedly and desperately to no avail.)* Bang, bang, bang, dammit! See! *(Shaking the gun furiously.)* How terribly disappointing!

RICHARD. *(Shaking hands.)* Hello, *(To Clarke.)* Mr. Van Kipness, *(To Beau.)* Mr. Van Kipness. I think you have a lovely home here.

BEAU. As do I.

CLARKE. As do I!

RICHARD. So sorry to have disrupted your Monday morning. I was in a bit of a temper when I found Dierdre's note. I'm sure you can understand.

BEAU. Dierdre, I thought you said he was large.

DIERDRE. He's larger than me.

RICHARD. Quite average, really.

BEAU. You seem charming for a serial killer.

RICHARD. I'm afraid to disappoint, but Dierdre's correct. I have not been entirely truthful.

DIERDRE. He's a liar and a fraud!

RICHARD. Indeed, I do take full responsibility for those accusations. I'm shamed to say I made up tales of brute strength and violence to frighten Dierdre from leaving me.

BEAU. That seems a rather risky plan.

CLARKE. You pretended to be a murderer?

RICHARD. To be honest, I assumed she knew it was all a game.

DIERDRE. How would I know?

SYLVIA. She doesn't appear to be an expert on games, darling.

RICHARD. Well, the stories were ridiculous, Dierdre. Honestly, it's impossible to rip a man's heart out with a teaspoon.

DIERDRE. You said it was serrated!

RICHARD. Just for theatricality.

DIERDRE. This is absurd! How do I know you're not lying now?

RICHARD. I suppose you just have to trust me.

DIERDRE. But that's just it! I don't trust you at all!

BEAU. If the chaps weren't dead, what prevented them from showing up again?

RICHARD. Well, first I scared them.

BEAU. By showing up at their homes with a large, slightly loaded rifle?

RICHARD. That is one of my most effective tactics, yes.

BEAU. And then—when you didn't actually kill them?

RICHARD. I paid them off.

BEAU. Ah.

DIERDRE. With money?

RICHARD. That is generally *how* you pay people off.

DIERDRE. But you haven't got any money.

RICHARD. I have. *(Deeply embarrassed.)* I just save it to bribe the men I've pretended to murder.

CLARKE. *(Calling upstairs.)* Marjorie! You can come down. No murderers, only lunatics.

DIERDRE. But, Richard! Perhaps if you'd spent that money on me—sweets, flowers, jewelry—I wouldn't have strayed in the first place!

SYLVIA. Excellent point, Dierdre.

RICHARD. But you never loved me Dierdre. Money would never have really mattered. I always knew you'd only married me to avoid your circumstances.

DIERDRE. *(Fearfully.)* Richard, don't. *(Trying to convince.)* I loved you…

RICHARD. Come now, Dierdre.

DIERDRE. *(On the same note.)* …a little.

BEAU. Circumstances?

DIERDRE. *(Utterly casual.)* It's nothing.

RICHARD. Haven't you told Beau how we met?

DIERDRE. Please, Richard.

BEAU. *(Concerned.)* No, she has not.

SYLVIA. *(Intrigued.)* No, she has not.

> *Marjorie enters, interrupting.*

MARJORIE. *(Cautious.)* No, she has not, what?

CLARKE. There you are darling!

MARJORIE. Hello.

SYLVIA. William, this is Marjorie.

MARJORIE. William?

SYLVIA. Richard! I'm sorry! Richard, this is Beau's wife, Marjorie.

RICHARD. Pleasure.

MARJORIE. I'm not sure I can return the compliment. *(Accusatorially.)* Are you here to kill my husband?

RICHARD. Not at all.

MARJORIE. *(Relieved.)* Well then. That's settled. I'm starving! Pardon me please.

> *Marjorie exits to the kitchen.*

BEAU. Sylvia, did you not call us in here to tell us some news.

SYLVIA. Oh heavens! Yes. The telephone.

CLARKE. I thought I heard it ring.

SYLVIA. *(Calling off.)* Marjorie! Bring your feast in here, dear, there's something I really must tell you.

MARJORIE. *(From off.)* Coming!

BEAU. Is everything alright?

SYLVIA. No, darling.

CLARKE. You have me quite anxious.

SYLVIA. *(Offering from yet another unlikely spot.)* Cigarette?

> *All ad-lib as they pull cigarettes from a variety of yet-revealed disguised cigarette holders. (I.e., Dierdre's cleavage, a large potted plant, a globe, a Fabergé egg, etc.)*

ALL. *(Ad-libbing while lighting up.)* No thanks./Got one./I'm fine. *(Etc.)*

> *Sylvia notices Dierdre, who still brandishes the gun.*

SYLVIA. Honestly, Dierdre, must you continue to wave that thing in the air?

DIERDRE. I haven't made up my mind if I believe him or not.

SYLVIA. Does it make a difference if I tell you that I do?

DIERDRE. *(Considering.)* Alright, I'll set it down but I'm keeping it close.

> *She sets it down. (Perhaps it fits perfectly in her cleavage or an unlikely decorative object near her—i.e., it rests atop a stuffed fish on the wall, or in the antlers of a hung deer head behind her.)*

SYLVIA. It's *not* loaded.

DIERDRE. *(A quote she's heard.)* "Better to have an ineffective weapon than no weapon at all."

SYLVIA. *(To Richard.)* Where on earth did you find this girl?

Marjorie enters with a tiered tray full of food.

MARJORIE. *(Moving to sit.)* Here.

SYLVIA. Right then. Marjorie, take a seat, dear. Are you all comfortable?

CLARKE. Oh, out with it Sylvia!

SYLVIA. Very well. I'm afraid…I'm afraid, that was Dr. Kent on the telephone. Mama has passed away.

Silence.

She died in her sleep this morning. I'm so sorry Clarke. Beau.

CLARKE. Mama—dead?

BEAU. I suppose we knew it was coming.

CLARKE. That doesn't make it any less of a shock.

BEAU. True.

CLARKE. Oh, brother!

The two brothers embrace.

MARJORIE. If it's a girl, we'll name the baby Beatrice.

SYLVIA. How thoughtful.

CLARKE. *(To Beau, still emotional.)* Have you got her papers, Beau? Her will?

BEAU. Not even in the ground, Clarke, and you're already counting her money? For shame.

CLARKE. *(Breaking out of the embrace and showing his true colors.)* Come now, we both know she was foul tempered and unloving. Why pretend?

DIERDRE. Pretend! Ha! Did she pretend she was a murderer?!

SYLVIA. Dierdre, dear, here. Have a drink.

Sylvia hands Dierdre a bottle of liquor.

Dierdre opens the bottle and, during the following dialogue, drinks straight from it—preferably without stopping at all—

until it is empty and she is very, very drunk. (This works best if the audience can see the liquid in the bottle disappear.)

Unbeknownst to all the others, the focus throughout the following dialogue is on Dierdre's miraculous effort of downing an entire bottle of liquid without pause while physically transforming from an upper-crust lady to an inebriated tramp (a long, slow slump from her upright position to nearly flat on the floor).

(Back to Beau and Clarke.) I don't think now is the time to disparage your mother.

MARJORIE. Right you are, Sylvia.

SYLVIA. Her disposition was a requirement of her station really. She was quite engaging if you took the time to speak with her.

BEAU. Engaging?!

CLARKE. Mother?!

SYLVIA. Well, yes—in her way. With her eclectic travels and her suffragette pamphlets. I always thought she was a woman ahead of her time.

MARJORIE. Mm, I see that.

BEAU. Complicated priorities for a mother of two boys growing up under the reign of Queen Victoria, wouldn't you say?

SYLVIA. The philosophy of the monarchy wasn't her concern, now was it?

BEAU. But she wanted nothing to do with us!

SYLVIA. Perhaps it was the demands of motherhood she took issue with, and not you specifically.

CLARKE. Regardless of her "issues," can I help it if I'd like to know whom she has left her fortune to? After all, I've got a baby on the way.

BEAU. Up until about an hour ago, I thought it was *I* who had a baby on the way.

MARJORIE. But you never wanted it.

BEAU. Why is it that women are constantly assuming my wants?

CLARKE. All I'm saying is this cottage is a lovely home in which to raise a child.

MARJORIE. You wanted a child, Beau?

BEAU. I wanted…I wanted…I wanted whatever life you wanted. And when I thought that meant a child, then yes, yes, then yes, that was the life I wanted.

MARJORIE. But did *you* want a child?

BEAU. I grew used to the idea, yes, I did.

MARJORIE. Don't you see the difference?

BEAU. What does it matter?

MARJORIE. It matters to me.

CLARKE. And to me!

> *They unite.*

MARJORIE. It matters to us!

CLARKE. In fact, it matters so much to us, that we wish to raise the child in the home I was raised in.

BEAU. Do you think Mama has left this cottage to you? Remember Clarke, I was raised here too.

CLARKE. Well, whomever she's left it to, Marjorie and I could make a happy home here.

MARJORIE. Oh, Clarke.

BEAU. Could you? Well, Dierdre and I could be quite happy here as well, couldn't we darling.

> *Their focus shifts to Dierdre and her empty bottle.*

DIERDRE. *(Drunk beyond drunk.)* Yesssss…

> *As she speaks she lands with a thud on the floor.*

BEAU. Dierdre!

> *Beau moves to her and props her up.*

RICHARD. That's why I never allowed her to drink.

CLARKE. Yes, you and Dierdre would be happy here, Beau. She seems like a bushel of laughs.

> *Beau moves to address Clarke, thus releasing Dierdre, who falls once more with a thud to the ground.*

BEAU. Now see here…

SYLVIA. Boys! Need I remind you, your mother has only just died. Show a little respect.

CLARKE. You're right Sylvia.

SYLVIA. A little decorum, please.

Dierdre moans and/or hiccups horribly.

CLARKE. I'm sorry, Beau. This has been an awfully tense morning.

BEAU. I agree.

SYLVIA. Poor dear. She's had a bit of a shock.

BEAU. I think we all have.

SYLVIA. Might we try to get unfortunate Dierdre off the floor, gentlemen?

The three men ad-lib ("Oh, of course," "Certainly," "You grab her middle," "Marjorie, do you mind?" Etc.) as they heave Dierdre off the floor...

RICHARD. Heave, ho.

...and onto the sofa (displacing disgruntled—"Well I never!"— still-eating Marjorie).

In the setting down of Dierdre, it becomes apparent to Clarke that she is rather inappropriately exposed. In a subtle effort to cover her up, Clarke sheepishly pulls Dierdre's skirt back down and maybe sets a pillow or a nearby hat over her exposed undergarments. (Perhaps there is fun to be had here with Richard's previously discarded beard/mustache/hair/hat.)

BEAU. *(Re: Dierdre's unladylike pose.)* Richard, what was that earlier about Dierdre's circumstances?

SYLVIA. *(With renewed curiosity.)* Oh. Yes?

RICHARD. Who am I to speak about Dierdre, Beau?

BEAU. Well, for starters, you're her husband.

RICHARD. Ex-husband.

BEAU. Right.

Richard gestures to passed out, exposed Dierdre.

RICHARD. She's yours now, Beau. You can find your circumstances together.

SYLVIA. *(Applauding.)* Bravo!

BEAU. You're suddenly chipper.

SYLVIA. Am I?

CLARKE. Yes, Sylvie. I noticed it too. You seem somehow less jilted.

SYLVIA. Well, it's not every day your husband leaves you for your lover's wife, is it? I suppose it's an adventure, really.

RICHARD. Oh Sylvie, I wish I'd known you were unhappy.

SYLVIA. I didn't really know I was.

> *Just then, Marjorie, who has been facing upstage, perhaps holding on to the banister, turns, screams, and grabs her belly.*

MARJORIE. Oooooooooohhhhhhhhhhhh!

> *Beau and Clarke rush to her side.*

CLARKE. Darling? Darling are you alright?

BEAU. Sylvie, call Dr. Porter at once!

SYLVIA. The least you could do is say please.

> *Marjorie grabs a nearby vase and starts to come at Sylvia, who narrowly escapes her.*

MARJORIE. *(Pained.)* FUCKING Pleeeeaaaase!

> *Sylvia crosses to the telephone.*

SYLVIA. You two are perfect for each other. Vases are your answer to everything.

MARJORIE. Clarke! Clarke! This is it! The baby's coming.

CLARKE. Are you certain?

MARJORIE. Certain as I'll ever be. Oooooooooooooooh.

> *Clarke's nerves get the better of him and he remains myopic throughout this ensuing hubbub. Ad-libbing (into the phone) "Run You Bastard!" (to the others) "I'm not ready for this!" Etc. As Beau and Richard tend to Clarke, Marjorie moans.*

SYLVIE. *(Into the phone, politely, loudly/simultaneously over the hoopla below.)* Hello, yes, this is Mrs. Van Kipness calling for Dr. Porter. My sister-in-law has gone into labor at the cottage. Can you send for him please.

MARJORIE. *(Moaning—in active labor.)* I need to lie down. Move this hammered hussy off the sofa!

> As Clarke mumbles myopically, Beau and Richard talk at once as they roll Dierdre off the sofa and onto the table.

BEAU. *(Ad-lib/freely.)* Yes, of course, darling, you must lie down. I'll grab her legs, sir, you take the rest of her. This is rather exciting, isn't it? I've never been present for the birth of a baby. I'm to be an uncle. That's rather grand isn't it. *(Etc.)*

RICHARD. *(Ad-lib/freely.)* Oh, of course, lying down is a good idea, though I always heard kneeling was the best position for childbirth, though I s'pose you're not asking for my midwifery expertise now are you. *(Etc.)*

CLARKE. *(Having spilled a glass of water on himself.)* I think my water broke!

> Now, Beau and Richard rush to help Clarke onto the sofa instead of Marjorie as the hubbub continues.

BEAU. I'm here for you brother! Don't be a sissy! Buck up, Clarke! *(Etc.)*

RICHARD. Good Lord, let's help the poor fellow. Bit of a dandy, isn't he? Can I get you a cigarette? *(Etc.)*

> Throughout the above utter mayhem, Dierdre manages to roll completely off of the table and onto the floor while she remains passed out.

> Beau and Richard's attention is entirely on pampering Clarke (fanning his brow, lighting him a cigarette, ad-libbing throughout, etc.) all while Marjorie continues to moan in labor until:

MARJORIE. Here she comes!

> And then—Marjorie passes gas. A loud, long eruption.

> After a beat of realization, as her explosion continues (in fits and starts), the others deliberately make their way away from the source.

> Clarke moves to the door (perhaps he even takes his hat and exits), Richard makes his way to the window, opens it a crack, and sticks his head (full body?) outside to get some air,

Beau makes his way to light a match, Sylvia covers her nose with the telephone mouthpiece, etc.

Finally, it ends. Nope. One final toot.

Dierdre, passed out on the ground, drunkenly waves her hand in front of her nose to swat away the stink.

And then...

(*Regaining composure.*) Sorry. Better now.

They all begin to restore themselves.

SYLVIE. (*Into the phone.*) Never mind, Mrs. Porter. That was an epic false alarm. Have a lovely Monday.

She hangs up the phone. Perhaps, if Clarke has managed to exit entirely, she lets him back in.

Always setting the bar for ladylike etiquette, Marjorie?

MARJORIE. I do apologize everyone. I suppose I shouldn't have eaten so quickly.

BEAU. (*Lighting a match to stave off the smell.*) Not exactly the *delivery* we had in mind.

CLARKE. (*Quite the Nervous Nancy—approaching Marjorie.*) My heart is still pounding. I thought the moment when I become a father had arrived.

MARJORIE. Calm down, Clarke.

SYLVIA. (*Through laughter.*) Clarke, better steer clear or else you're at risk of being blown away by the British Bomber.

MARJORIE. Must you be so crass?

SYLVIA. Me?! You just joined ranks with sailors of the Royal Navy! Aren't I right, William?

Richard and Sylvia laugh.

MARJORIE. William, again. Which is it, sir? Are you Richard or William?

Sylvia bites her tongue. A beat.

BEAU. Your silence, sir, does nothing for your cause.

RICHARD. (*Requesting permission.*) Sylvia?

SYLVIA. Alright. Only wait a moment. If you're going to come clean, your wife should be conscious.

Sylvia gets a glass of water as the dialogue continues.

RICHARD. Ex-wife.

CLARKE. Come clean with what?

SYLVIA. Look, this day has been a barrage of betrayal and I'm exhausted from it. I, for one, cannot stand idly by while my ex-lover's lover's husband...

RICHARD. Ex-husband...

SYLVIA. ...announces his secret identity while his wife...

RICHARD. Ex-wife...

SYLVIA. ...lies drunk on my dead mother-in-law's carpet. It's just too much for one morning, really.

CLARKE. This carpet no longer belongs to Mama.

BEAU. Cataloging the furniture, Clarke?!

SYLVIA. Not now gentlemen! Hang on.

Now face to face with Dierdre, Sylvia throws the cup of water into Dierdre's face. Dierdre audibly startles, but is still rather unconscious.

Sorry, Dierdre.

Sylvia has now lifted Dierdre up into a seated position and smacks her squarely across the face!

DIERDRE. Ow!

SYLVIA. Good morning, darling. Ready to join the party?

DIERDRE. *(Slurred and perky.)* Oh! Is there a party?

SYLVIA. *(Trying to stand Dierdre up.)* It never stopped.

DIERDRE. Will there be games?

SYLVIA. C'mon, stand up.

Richard helps Sylvia get poor, wet Dierdre to her feet.

DIERDRE. *(Coming to a bit—then furiously refusing Richard's support.)* Get your hands off me!

SYLVIA. Oh good! You're awake. Splendid. *(Then.)* Beau, would you mind terribly getting Dierdre a glass of water?

BEAU. Pleasure.

Beau moves to get water.

SYLVIA. Dierdre, stand here, dear. There's something Richard would like to tell you.

DIERDRE. *(Slurred still.)* I'm not interested in an apology, sir.

RICHARD. You're right, Dierdre, I do owe you an apology. Though, that's not what I have to say.

DIERDRE. *(Interrupting.)* How much money?

RICHARD. Sorry?

DIERDRE. *(Accusingly.)* How much money have you spent over the years buying my lovers' silence?

RICHARD. Too much to count, I'm afraid.

DIERDRE. As much as you spent to buy me?!

RICHARD. Dierdre!

DIERDRE. *(Drunkenly to the room.)* I'm a prostitute you know?!

SYLVIA. *(To Richard.)* You married a prostitute?!

RICHARD. I was lonely, Sylvie. It was impossible to fill the void after…

DIERDRE. After what?!

Beau emerges with a cup of water.

BEAU. What's going on?

MARJORIE. My husband's been sleeping with a prostitute!

BEAU. *(To Dierdre.)* You said you worked in hospitality!

RICHARD. That's a word for it.

SYLVIA. *(Ruefully.)* You should have told me, William!

CLARKE. Sylvie, do you two know each other?

SYLVIA. Just let him explain.

BEAU. Yes, will someone please explain.

RICHARD. There was a brothel in my neighborhood.

DIERDRE. *(With enormous Cockney pride.)* My mother's brothel. Best brothel in London.

SYLVIA. It's impolite to boast, Dierdre.

RICHARD. I started going there every so often, to stave off the loneliness.

CLARKE. I know the feeling.

MARJORIE. You do?!

CLARKE. That's what drew me to you, darling. I was so dangerously lonely with Sylvia.

RICHARD. Funny. I was so lonely without her.

BEAU. It seems clear now that we've all been lonely either with or without Sylvia.

> *A beat.*

But the question remains, who are you, sir.

DIERDRE. This is my husband, Richard.

RICHARD. Ex-husband. And my name is William Pierce.

DIERDRE. *(With extreme relief.)* Oh thank God! You look so much like my husband, the murderer.

RICHARD. Dierdre, I am your husband the murderer. Only I'm not your husband anymore, I never murdered anyone, and my name is William Pierce.

> *As Dierdre begins to (loudly—"ahhh") faint again, Sylvia props her back up.*

SYLVIA. Darling, you really must stay awake for this.

RICHARD. And I'm in love with Sylvia.

SYLVIA. William!

> *Sylvia thoughtlessly releases Dierdre. As Dierdre falls, Clarke stands.*

CLARKE. William! William?! From your father's apothecary?!

SYLVIA. Can you believe it?!

> *Beau finds himself a drink in an unlikely place while dialogue continues.*

RICHARD. I've been in love with you all this time but never thought I'd see you again; let alone have the opportunity to declare my love for you wholeheartedly.

SYLVIA. Oh William!

He kisses her passionately.

CLARKE. Sylvia said you were dead.

She breaks the kiss to reply.

SYLVIA. I thought he was!

He resumes their kiss.

DIERDRE. My Richard is your William?!

Sylvia breaks the kiss again, with concern.

SYLVIA. But, you let me think you were dead.

DIERDRE. Ha! I told you they both had green eyes!

SYLVIA. But, you've been alive.

Dierdre totters her way to Beau.

DIERDRE. Well, two can play at that game?

SYLVIA. And you're married to a prostitute!

RICHARD. *(A quick correction.)* Used to be married.

He tries to kiss her again, but she is wary.

MARJORIE. The divorce does not negate the marriage.

DIERDRE. C'mere, Beau my beast.

Dierdre snuggles up to Beau.

BEAU. You lied to me. And you smell.

Beau moves away from Dierdre (who falls to the ground) and goes to the bar to fix himself a drink.

DIERDRE. *(From the ground.)* I didn't lie to you any more than you lied to me! You've got a pregnant wife!

MARJORIE and CLARKE. It's not his.

BEAU. *(Wiping his brow.)* I'm afraid I'm not feeling well.

He takes a swig.

SYLVIA. Neither am I.

She takes a swig of Beau's drink.

DIERDRE. *(To Beau.)* Oh, come on! Don't be cross, darling. Let our lies cancel each other out! The game is all tied up.

BEAU. This isn't a game!

DIERDRE. You said it was!

BEAU. Well, I'm no longer playing! *(Entitled.)* I've followed the rules my entire life and look where it's got me!

A beat.

CLARKE. Followed the rules?! Of brotherhood?

MARJORIE. Of marriage?!

SYLVIA. Of love?!

DIERDRE. *(Earnestly.)* Oh no. He broke all those rules.

BEAU. Yes, well… Sylvia, congratulations on finding a lost, dead, love. I hope you'll be happy. Richard, or William, whomever you are, thank you for not murdering me. Marjorie, I wish you the best with the birth of…your child. Clarke, we'll have the funeral to arrange, so perhaps we can discuss it in my office first thing tomorrow morning.

CLARKE. That's what I was going to say!

Beau, irritated, repeats Clarke's last line in an immature imitation as he moves to exit to the bedroom.

Dierdre, sobering up a bit, gets up and goes to him.

DIERDRE. But what about me?

BEAU. What about you?

DIERDRE. Where shall I go?

BEAU. Wherever you like.

DIERDRE. Well, I'd like to go with you.

BEAU. You may take the train with me if you like. But I'm afraid this is the end of our ride, Dierdre.

DIERDRE. But, what will you do? No wife? No sister-in-law? No me?

She's quite right. Beau straightens himself up.

BEAU. That, my dear, is no concern of yours.

DIERDRE. *(Pulling papers from her cleavage—oh, yes, they've been there all along.)* But I've got my divorce papers.

BEAU. I never suggested you get divorced. *(To Marjorie.)* Just as I never told you I didn't want a child. *(To Sylvia.)* Just as I never asked you to send a telegram.

CLARKE. You didn't?

BEAU. No. My wife is expecting after all.

MARJORIE. And now that you know what you know, would you still have it that way? Married to me, raising your brother's child, all the while having a sordid love affair with a married prostitute, and one recurring date per year with your brother's wife, who's in love with another man, who may or may not be a murderer?

BEAU. *(Uncharacteristically foul tempered.)* Yes! I thought that was perfectly lovely, thank you! *(Then.)* Now, if you'll excuse me, I'm going to make myself a cup of tea.

> *Beau exits to the kitchen. A moment passes and then Dierdre begins to sob.*

SYLVIA. Come now, Dierdre, isn't this where we began?

DIERDRE. But what's to become of me?

SYLVIA. Do you really want to build a life with a man who's been dishonest with you? *(A realization.)* Oh…

DIERDRE. What?

SYLVIA. That's quite a good question, isn't it? *(Handing her a hanky.)* Here. Wipe your tears.

RICHARD. You'll find another chap, sweetheart. *(From experience.)* You always do.

DIERDRE. That's true. *(A realization—then an attempt—to Clarke.)* You're looking awfully sharp.

MARJORIE. Not in this room, dear.

DIERDRE. Right. Of course. Sorry. *(Starting to cry.)* Oh what's the use! I'll never find another man like Beau!

SYLVIA. Perhaps you don't need a man.

> *They all gasp!*

ALL. Sylvie!

> *If there were a lightbulb above Sylvia's head, it would turn on.*

SYLVIA. Well? Perhaps she doesn't. Are these gentlemen not to be held accountable? Is our bad behavior not merely a reaction to their own?

MARJORIE. Oh my, Sylvie.

SYLVIA. Why should Dierdre have to live her life steeped in the lies of men?

DIERDRE. *(Tearful.)* I thought he was my destiny.

RICHARD. Perhaps he is.

DIERDRE. No, no, he's not, don't you see?! He's not at all in love with *me.*

RICHARD. But what's that to do with whether or not he's your destiny?

DIERDRE. I'm not his.

RICHARD. Is that a requirement of soul mates? Reciprocity?

DIERDRE. Isn't it?

SYLVIA. Excellent question.

MARJORIE. I've never thought of it.

CLARKE. Unrequited love is not a new phenomenon.

DIERDRE. So what? People just go through life bumping into each other, hoping eventually to meet the one person who'll complete them, but all the while, odds are that if they do meet that one person, it will be for naught, because that person, turns out, is not at all looking for them?

RICHARD. Precisely.

DIERDRE. *(Sobbing.)* How miserable.

RICHARD. Not entirely. Plenty of people lead perfectly happy lives opposite someone who is most assuredly intended for someone else.

MARJORIE. Happy you say?

RICHARD. Well, yes. Mostly.

DIERDRE. But if shared true love is such a rarity, then what's the point of searching at all?

RICHARD. The game of it, really.

DIERDRE. *(With renewed spirit.)* Mm. Yes. I do love games.

SYLVIA. Is that what all this is to you, William? A game?

RICHARD. Well, no...I...

SYLVIA. I thought you were dead.

RICHARD. I…

SYLVIA. I've thought your ghost has come to me in dreams.

DIERDRE. Ghosts are so scary.

SYLVIA. Your death was not at all a game to me. And now, I come to learn that the one person—that I thought was destined for me, was actually alive and well, married to a prostitute.

DIERDRE. You don't need to keep bringing that up. I had limited options. *(Pointed at Marjorie.)* Not everybody's born a baroness.

    At this Beau reenters holding tea.

MARJORIE. *(Shocked.)* Beau told you about me?!

    Without a word, Beau spins on a dime and exits back into the kitchen.

DIERDRE. Only in that he had a frosty baroness for a wife.

    Marjorie gasps, furious.

SYLVIA. Welcome to the party, Marj.

RICHARD. Sylvia, I've loved you all this time, imagining us, at seventeen, many a night.

SYLVIA. But, we're not seventeen anymore, are we? Quite far from it, in fact. You've allowed my entire youth to pass me by.

DIERDRE. And now she's old.

SYLVIA. *(A beat to absorb the insult.)* Thank you, Dierdre. *(Back to Richard.)* All those years I've mourned you. I'll never get those back. I'm changed now, William. I'm a grown woman.

RICHARD. But, I still love you.

SYLVIA. I'm not sure that matters. *(A realization.)* Good Lord!

ALL. What?

SYLVIA. I'm truly on my own now, aren't I?

CLARKE and RICHARD. Well, I…

SYLVIA. No! Enough. No more charades.

DIERDRE. Oooo! I love charades! Let's play! I've got a good one! *(Thrilled with herself.)* Guess what I'm doing.

    Dierdre begins to elaborately act out "having an affair." The others, except Sylvia, really get into it, guessing ridiculously.

"Cooking." "Race car driving." "King Tut's burial chamber." "You're an Irish nationalist." "You're Santa Claus." "You're Mary Pickford." "Tobogganing." Etc.

Beau enters, an envelope in his hand. Throughout the following he opens the envelope and reads the contents.

Dierdre runs to Beau and begins to elaborately act out "having an affair."

BEAU. *(Rebuking her advances.)* Don't!

DIERDRE. No, no, darling! I'm "acting"! I'm pretending to "have an affair."

All (Except Beau and Sylvia) join in with, "Ohhh!" "Is that what you were doing?" "Yes, I see it now." "Jolly good." "You're quite the little actress." Etc.

BEAU. No more games! I've got a train to catch.

CLARKE. Yes, well, I suppose we ought to catch the train as well.

MARJORIE. Yes, I'd like to get home to a bath.

CLARKE. Funny.

MARJORIE. What?

CLARKE. Whose home shall you return to?

MARJORIE. Oh. Hadn't thought of that.

CLARKE. Sylvie?

SYLVIA. Hmm?

CLARKE. Is it alright with you if Marjorie comes to our home for a while?

SYLVIA. Do you mean forever?

CLARKE. Yes, I suppose I do.

MARJORIE. Oh, Clarke.

SYLVIA. Yes, Clarke. I won't be there any longer.

CLARKE. Well then, we will.

MARJORIE. Indeed.

They kiss.

DIERDRE. *(To Sylvia.)* But where will you go?

SYLVIA. I don't know. *(Thoughtfully—a quote.)* Mama always said, "A woman needs her own space to hear herself think."

DIERDRE. *(To Richard.)* And where will you go? To our flat?

RICHARD. No. I don't plan to return there.

DIERDRE. Oooh! Can I have it then?

RICHARD. I don't see why not.

DIERDRE. Really?

RICHARD. It was my hiding spot.

DIERDRE. From what?

RICHARD. Myself, I s'pose. But—I've no need to hide anymore.

DIERDRE. You know, if you really aren't a murderer, then you are quite a nice man.

RICHARD. Thank you.

DIERDRE. Well, then I suppose I will take the train back with you all.

CLARKE. This is bound to be a fun train ride.

DIERDRE. Maybe we can play more charades to pass the time!

BEAU. Splendid.

MARJORIE. I'll just use the loo before we go.

> *Ad-libs of agreement. ("Jolly good idea." "Oh yes, please do." "Couldn't hurt, Marj." "For the love of God." Etc.)*

> *Marjorie, midexit, absorbs the insult, and then carries on to the bathroom.*

DIERDRE. I'll get our coats.

> *Dierdre exits to the guest room.*

BEAU. Before we leave, there is the matter of the cottage.

CLARKE. This cottage?

BEAU. The very same.

CLARKE. I thought you said we weren't to discuss it.

BEAU. I did. But then I found this *(Re: the envelope.)*, addressed to us, in the kitchen…

CLARKE. Is that her will?

BEAU. Left in a tin of biscuits. It's all as we suspected. Everything split evenly down the middle.

CLARKE. So then, we're to share the cottage.

BEAU. All as we suspected, except for one thing. Read here.

Beau points to a spot on the will.

CLARKE. *(Reading.)* "In the matter of the family cottage situated in Moreton in Marsh, I leave full ownership to my daughter-in-law, Sylvia Ann Markinson Van Kipness." *(Then.)* To Sylvia?

SYLVIA. *(Joyfully shocked.)* Hoorah.

DIERDRE. *(Upon reentering.)* What's just happened?

SYLVIA. Dear old Mama has left this cottage, my most favorite place in all the world, to me!!!

CLARKE. *(Finding the loophole.)* But Sylvia is my wife, so therefore in truth I own…

BEAU. Keep reading.

CLARKE. *(Reading.)* "In the event that my son, Clarke Van Kipness, should divorce Sylvia Ann Markinson Van Kipness, ownership of said property shall remain…Sylvia's." *(Then.)* That bitch.

BEAU. Careful.

CLARKE. We're not divorced yet!

SYLVIA. Oh Clarke, really? After all this, you expect me to stay married to you so that you can play house here with Marjorie and a baby?

DIERDRE. That is a bit much to ask, Clarke.

CLARKE. Gah! *(To Sylvia.)* None of this would have ever happened had you not sent those blasted telegrams!

BEAU. A will is a will, Clarke, telegrams or no.

DIERDRE. It was predestined!

CLARKE. Don't you speak to me of destiny!

BEAU. Don't you speak to her about what she can speak to you of!

CLARKE. Don't you speak to me about what I can speak to her to speak to me of!

Sylvia, quiet till now, refers to a portrait of Mama.

SYLVIA. She knew.

BEAU, CLARKE, DIERDRE, and RICHARD. Knew what?

> *Sylvia relays this story almost as a bedtime tale. The others gather around. Once more, a family moment.*

SYLVIA. We were at a summer picnic, all of us, a few years ago, and she turned to me and said, "I didn't know you and Clarke visited the cottage last week. I found your pearl-and-sapphire earrings." Only we hadn't, see. I had been here for my one night with you.

BEAU. So what did you say?

SYLVIA. I don't know why really, perhaps I couldn't bear lying to an old woman, but I just came out with it.

CLARKE. You told her?

SYLVIA. I said, "I didn't visit the cottage with Clarke. I was there with Beau."

BEAU. No!

SYLVIA. Yes.

DIERDRE. And what did *she* say?

SYLVIA. She smiled. In fact, it was the first time I'd ever seen her smile. And she said, *(Stately.)* "Ah. Then, I see you've discovered what the cottage is for."

> *Beau and Clarke nearly choke.*

CLARKE. Mother said that?!

SYLVIA. She might have been cold to you back in your home in London, but she'd obviously been quite warm with somebody right here.

CLARKE. Sylvia, really. You're talking about our mother as though she were nothing but a cheap prostitute.

DIERDRE. *(Deeply offended.)* Hey.

> *Marjorie enters.*

SYLVIA. Call her what you want, but your mother has left this cottage to me!

MARJORIE. Noooooo!

SYLVIA. Yesssss!

MARJORIE. Clarke?

CLARKE. I'm afraid it's true.

MARJORIE. Beau, can she do that?

BEAU. She can and she has.

MARJORIE. It's not fair!

Sylvia begins to laugh.

BEAU. What's so funny.

SYLVIA. Mama's done it.

BEAU. Done what?

SYLVIA. Killed two birds with one stone.

BEAU. I suppose my brother and I are the birds.

SYLVIA. Tweet, tweet, my sweet.

BEAU. Clever.

Richard, now William, is suddenly down on one knee.

WILLIAM. Sylvia…

Everyone gasps as they notice him in proposal position.

I've loved you since we were seventeen years old.

MARJORIE. Good Lord, is this a proposal?

DIERDRE. Shhh…

WILLIAM. I don't want to live another moment without you.

DIERDRE. *(Teary.)* How lovely.

WILLIAM. Live with me in this cottage forever. Marry me Sylvia Ann Markinson…

BEAU and CLARKE. Van Kipness.

WILLIAM. Van Kipness.

A moment of enormous hesitation.

SYLVIA. No.

ALL. No?

SYLVIA. *(Gently.)* No. I won't marry you, William. I've no idea who you are, really.

DIERDRE. Oh, he's my husband.

ALL. Ex-husband.

SYLVIA. But I know who I am.

WILLIAM, BEAU, and CLARKE. As do I.

SYLVIA. That's kind of you all. But, I think, perhaps, untrue.

DIERDRE. One can only know one's self, when one's self is free from the restraints others impose.

> *All look at her.*

Ha! That one just came to me just then.

SYLVIA. Thank you, Dierdre.

WILLIAM. What am I to do? I've found you. I can't lose you now.

SYLVIA. I wasn't ever lost, William.

WILLIAM. But…

SYLVIA. I'm sorry.

BEAU. And to think how this day began.

SYLVIA. Indeed.

DIERDRE. *(A final quote for the road.)* "Expectations only exist to be thwarted and replaced with reality."

> *All grumble at Dierdre. ("Yes, thank you," "I think that's enough now," etc.)*

SYLVIA. Right then. Well, it appears, our games are over.

> *On each other's heels…*

BEAU. Indeed.

CLARKE. Indeed.

WILLIAM. Indeed.

SYLVIA. *(Soaking in the cottage in a new light.)* You know, I've never really owned anything. Myself, I mean.

MARJORIE. Ownership is overrated.

SYLVIA. Green is not your color, Baroness.

MARJORIE. Honestly, Sylvia. What will you do alone in this cottage?

SYLVIA. *(Nearly giddy with possibility.)* Everything!

DIERDRE. If I had a cottage of my own, I think I'd like to paint.

SYLVIA. Do you paint, Dierdre?

DIERDRE. No. But, I think I would. If I had a cottage.

SYLVIA. Right. Well, maybe I'll paint.

MARJORIE. I want to paint!

DIERDRE. Ooo! Can we have a paint party?!

SYLVIA. Yes. Yes, ladies. We shall have a paint party.

DIERDRE. Oh goody! I can hardly wait!

SYLVIA. But, until then, I rather think I'll enjoy the solitude for a while.

MARJORIE. And the gardener?

BEAU and CLARKE. The gardener?

SYLVIA. *(With a twinkle.)* Ooo. I'd forgotten about him. Marji. What a grand idea.

MARJORIE. *(Relishing a memory.)* Yes, it was.

CLARKE. Marji?

MARJORIE. Hm?

SYLVIA. Right. Well then. I suppose it is now well within my rights to say…

> Sylvia opens the door. Wind blows, birds chirp.

…"Get Out!" You've all well worn out your welcome this morning.

BEAU. Aha. Well. That's it, then. Congratulations, Sylvia. It's no small feat to have won Mama's affection.

SYLVIA. I suppose we were kindred spirits.

BEAU. Perhaps what she always wanted was a daughter.

SYLVIA. Or her freedom. Goodbye, Beau. Good luck.

BEAU. So long, Sylvie.

SYLVIA. Oh, come now, once more for old times' sake.

BEAU. So long…Tulip.

SYLVIA. *(A moment of brief ecstasy.)* Ah. *(A return to propriety.)* That's it. Farewell, Beau.

> Beau exits.

(To the rest.) You've got to admit, he is good.

ALL. He is.

BEAU. *(Popping back in.)* Thank you.

   He's out again.

DIERDRE. *(Trying to figure it all out.)* What a funny morning.

WILLIAM. You could say that.

DIERDRE. Goodbye Richard.

WILLIAM. It's William now.

DIERDRE. Yes, well goodbye then. It's all been rather confusing.

WILLIAM. You'll sort it out. Goodbye, Dierdre.

   Dierdre has gathered her things.

DIERDRE. Goodbye Sylvia. It was a pleasure to meet you.

SYLVIA. Thank you for your wisdom, Dierdre.

DIERDRE. Wisdom? Me?

SYLVIA. Mmm.

DIERDRE. Oh. *(Earnestly.)* Well, you're welcome. *(With new-found confidence.)* Good day, everyone.

   Dierdre exits.

WILLIAM. Perhaps we could have supper tonight, Sylvia? Start again?

SYLVIA. I think not, William. Best for us to begin fresh on a new day, don't you think?

WILLIAM. I shall look forward to it.

SYLVIA. Yes. Goodbye then, William. I'm ever so glad you're not dead.

WILLIAM. Me too. Goodbye, Sylvia. Until we meet again.

   William exits, with a little bow.

MARJORIE. Well, we're off then.

   She moves to the door.

Try not to gloat, Sylvie. It doesn't suit you.

SYLVIA. Try not to fart, Marji. It's disgusting.

   She absorbs the sting and exits. Clarke moves to follow her.

CLARKE. *(Calling after her.)* Marjorie…

SYLVIA. Clarke. My Clarke. Well, we've had a time of it, haven't we?

CLARKE. You could say so.

SYLVIA. We had some laughs.

CLARKE. I suppose we did.

SYLVIA. Thank you, Clarke. For everything.

CLARKE. I'm sorry it didn't work out between us.

SYLVIA. I never meant to make you lonely.

She kisses him gently on the cheek.

CLARKE. So long, Sylvie. Good luck.

SYLVIA. Thank you.

Clarke exits calling after "Marji!" Sylvia stands in the open doorway watching them go. Finally, she shuts the door. She screams for joy!

(To the portrait of Mama.) Oh, Mama! We've done it! You nasty woman! The cottage! Thank you!

Blackout.

End of Play

OR IS IT???

As an option, the blackout may be delayed, and the play may carry on as follows:

Suddenly, there's a knock at the door. Sylvia looks out—looks to the door.

SYLVIA. *(Calling from the sofa.)* Yes?

The door opens. A gorgeous gardener stands in the doorway.

GARDENER. 'Ello, Miss. 'Ere to trim your boxwoods and get into your pansies. Anything else you'd like me to do for you?

Sylvia looks out to the audience with delight as music plays and the curtain falls.

Blackout.

Note: The role of the gardener may be played by an additional actor or male understudy, or can function as an opportunity for an unexpected cameo appearance or a moment to shine for a member of the crew. If this option is put into action, it is best to disguise this role in the program, perhaps by listing a seventh name. (Oscar or Thomas or Cedric or...)

A note about the curtain call: Companies of THE COTTAGE should have fun with the bows. As 1920s dance music plays, cast members can enter from all entrances (even crawl in through the window)! Perhaps Clarke enters for his bow holding a baby! Perhaps Marjorie does too! (It was twins!)

After bowing, they can exit all together up to the bedroom, Dierdre grabbing some booze along her way, or perhaps each couple saunters off to different parts of the house, or maybe Sylvia doesn't notice as the others sneak their way back into the cottage, or maybe they all simply "Cheers" each other and dance the night away as the curtain falls. Anything goes?!

ALTERNATE LINE NOTES

The reference to eye color should be made specific to the actor playing William/Richard.

If the actor playing William/Richard is not particularly "tall," the line on page 45 may be changed to:

SYLVIA. William was kind. Kinder than your average boy. Broad shouldered. Brown eyed.

If the actor playing William/Richard is particularly "large," the following sequence on page 73 may be cut:

BEAU. Dierdre, I thought you said he was large.
DIERDRE. He's larger than me.
RICHARD. Quite average, really.

For a PG option on page 80, the line may be changed to:

MARJORIE. *(Pained.)* Pleeeeaaaase!

If Beau does not have his coat on when he exits off with Dierdre at the end of Act One, Dierdre's line on page 92 may be adjusted to:

DIERDRE. I'll get my coat.

PROPERTY LIST

(Use this space to create props lists for your production)

SOUND EFFECTS

(Use this space to create sound effects lists for your production)

Hello, actors, theatre makers, and theatre fans,

On behalf of Broadway Licensing Global and the author(s) of this work, we thank you for your continued support of the arts and the playwrights you love.

Like every title in our catalogue, this play is covered by copyright law, which ensures authors are rewarded for creating new dramatic work and protects them from theft and abuse of their work. We are compelled to impress upon all who obtain this edition that **this text may not be copied, distributed, or publicly produced in any way,** nor uploaded to any file-sharing websites or software—public or private. Any such action has an immediate and negative effect on the livelihood of the writer(s)—it is also stealing and is against the law. As a result, should you copy, distribute, or publicly produce any part of this text without express written consent and licensed permission from our company—even if no one is being paid and/or admission is not being charged—your organization shall be subject to legal consequences that we are sure you want to avoid.

But we have faith in you and your understanding of these guidelines!

While this acting edition is the only approved text for performance, there may be other editions of the play available for sale. It is important to note that our team has worked with the playwright(s) to ensure this published acting edition reflects their desired text for all future productions. If you have purchased a revised edition from us, that is the only edition you may use for performance, unless explicitly stated in writing by our team.

Finally, and this is an important one, **this script cannot be changed in any way** without written permission from our team. That said, feel free to reach out to us. We don't bite, and we are always happy to have a discussion to see if we can accommodate your request.

We are thrilled this play has made it into your hands and we hope you love it as much as we do. Thank you for helping us keep the theatre alive and well, and for supporting playwrights, in our continued journey to make everyone a theatre person!

Sincerely,
Fellow theatre lovers at Broadway Licensing Global

Note on Songs/Recordings, Images, or Other Production Design Elements

Be advised that Broadway Licensing neither holds the rights to nor grants permission to use any songs, recordings, images, or other design elements mentioned in the play. It is the responsibility of the producing theater/organization to obtain permission of the copyright owner(s) for any such use. Additional royalty fees may apply for the right to use copyrighted materials.

For any songs/recordings, images, or other design elements mentioned in the play, works in the public domain may be substituted. It is the producing theater/organization's responsibility to ensure the substituted work is indeed in the public domain. Broadway Licensing cannot advise as to whether or not a song/ arrangement/recording, image, or other design element is in the public domain.